THE STATE OF WORLD POPULATION 1999

6 Billion

A Time for Choices

UNFPA
United Nations
Population Fund

Dr. Nafis Sadik, Executive Director

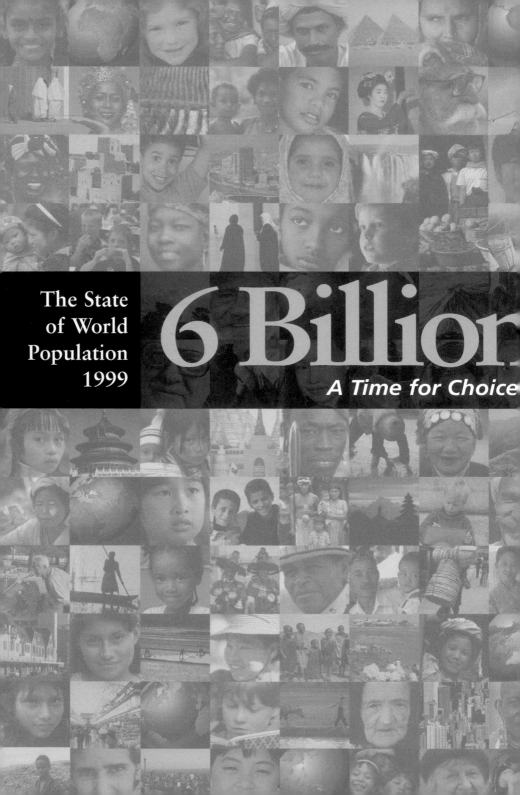

The State of World Population 1999

6 Billion

A Time for Choice

CONTENTS

CHAPTER 1

Overview and Introduction 1

Demographic Trends 4
ICPD: An Agenda for Choices.....................6
  Population and Development 9
  Reproductive and Sexual Health and Rights 11
  Gender Equality and Women's Empowerment....15
  Partnerships and Participation 17
  The Question of Resources 18
Going Forward 20

CHAPTER 2

Population Change and People's Choices 23

Population and Development: Changing Policies....24
Population Continues to Grow, and to
  Grow Older 28
  Death Rate Cut by Half......................29
  Fertility is Declining, but Unevenly 29
  Education Levels and Fertility Declines 32
  Ageing Populations 35
  The Youth Factor ....35.
  The Impact of AIDS............................37
  Prospects for Low-fertility Countries 37
Changing Distribution of World Population 38
  Regional Distribution Changing.....................38
  Global Trend Towards Urbanization 39
  International Migration 41
Population Growth and Environmental Concerns..42
  Water, Land and Food 42
  Climate Change, Natural Resource
  Degradation and Biodiversity 44

CHAPTER 3

Reproductive Health and Reproductive Rights 45

The Reproductive Health Approach 45
Components of Reproductive Health 47
  Family Planning 47
  Safe Motherhood 48
  HIV/AIDS and Sexually
  Transmitted Diseases........................51
  Female Genital Mutilation 53
Providing Reproductive Health Services 54
  Policy Change since the ICPD 54
  Health Sector Reform and Decentralization 55

Integrating and Broadening Reproductive
  Health Programmes......................................56
NGO Provision of Reproductive
  Health Services 58
Increasing Access to Quality Services 59
Communication and Education 62
Developing Human Resources 63
Monitoring and Evaluation 64
Information and Care for Adolescents...................65
Male Involvement and Responsibility 68
Reproductive Health for Refugees and
  Displaced Persons.............................69

CHAPTER 4

Partnership and Empowerment 71

The Emerging Vision of Civil Society 72
Empowerment, Gender Equality and
  Reproductive Rights...............................74
  Action for Women's Empowerment 74
  Reproductive Health and Rights Advocacy 74
  Combating Gender-based Violence...................75
Strength in Numbers: Networks and Alliances 76
Governments and Civil Society in Partnership........78
Collaboration with Other Sectors of Civil Society....80
  Religious Leaders 80
  Parliamentarians United for Reproductive
  Health and Rights 80
  The Private Sector 81
  Medical Associations 82
Strengthening Partnerships 83
  Current Constraints 83
UNFPA and NGOs 84

CHAPTER 5

Finding the Resources 87

Investing in Development 87
  The Resource Challenge....................88
  Increasing Resources 89
Where Does The Money Come from Now? 90
  External Assistance 90
  Domestic Resources 92
  Increasing Efficiency.......................93
Partnerships for Health 94
  Who Pays: How Should We Decide? 94
  Making Sure Reproductive Health
  Services Reach the Poor 96
Conclusion 97

NOTES 98

BOXES

1. Population May Grow to 8.9 Billion by 2050 3

2. Longer Lives + Falling Birth Rates =
   Slower Population Growth 5

3. Goals of the ICPD — and New Benchmarks......7

4. Countering Violence and Coercion
   Directed at Women 15

5. UNFPA: Building the Consensus......................21

6. Population and Development:
   New Conclusions 25

7. South-east Asian Crisis May Erase
   Development Progress 26

8. Lower Population Projections:
   Good News and Bad...30

9. Devastating Impact of HIV/AIDS in Africa......36

10. One Person in Four May Face
    Water Shortages by 2050 43

11. The Right to Reproductive Health 47

12. Japan Approves Use of Oral Contraceptives 49

13. ICPD Programme of Action on
    Unsafe Abortion 50

14. Combating STDs and HIV in Uganda.............52

15. Literacy Group Spurs Fight against
    FGM in Senegal 54

16. Health-sector Reform 56

17. Integration at the Service Delivery Level
    in Uganda 57

18. Using Peer Education to Reduce
    Adolescent Pregnancy 66

19. Teach Men about the Benefits of
    Family Planning 69

20. Rape is Commonplace in Kenyan
    Refugee Camp 70

21. UNFPA and Parliamentarians 81

22. Involving the Private Sector in Meeting
    Contraceptive Commodity Needs 82

23. Enabling Environment for
    Effective Partnership...85

24. Debt Relief and the Resource Challenge 89

CHARTS AND GRAPHS

Fig. 1: World Population Growth,
        Actual and Projected, 1950-2050 3

Fig. 2: Educational Attainment by Gender,
        Region..33

Fig. 3: Regional Trends in Age Structure 34

Fig. 4: The Impact of AIDS in Sub-Saharan Africa:
        Population Projections with and without
        AIDS in the 29 Most-affected Countries,
        1980-2050 36

Fig. 5: Regional Distribution of Population,
        1950-2050..40

Fig. 6: World Urbanization Trends,
        1950-2030..41

Fig. 7: Percentage of Sexually Active,
        Never-Married, Young Women, 15-19,
        Using Family Planning, Selected Countries 65

TABLES

Measures Taken to Develop Partnerships
    with Civil Society 73

Public and Private Health Expenditure 94

INDICATORS

Monitoring ICPD Goals —
    Selected Indicators 108

Demographic, Social and
    Economic Indicators...118

Selected Indicators for
    Less-Populous Countries/Territories 128

Notes for Indicators 130

Technical Notes..131

CHAPTER 1

Overview and Introduction

UNICEF / 714 / Nicole Toutounji

On 12 October 1999, 6 billion people will be alive in the world, an addition of a billion in only 12 years. Nearly half will be under 25; over a billion will be young people between 15 and 24, the parents of the next generation.

World population is growing at 78 million a year, a little less than the total population of Germany. It has doubled since 1960. Over 95 per cent of population growth is in developing countries. Meanwhile, population growth has slowed or stopped in Europe, North America and Japan. The United States is the only industrial country where large population increases are still projected, largely as the result of immigration.

Reaching 6 billion has both positive and negative aspects. On the positive side, it is the result of personal choice and collective action for better health and longer life. This is reflected, for example, in:

Every newborn whose mother had a healthy pregnancy;

Every infant who is properly fed and immunized;

Every girl who receives better nutrition, health care and education;

Every young woman who can protect herself from HIV infection;

Every woman who can space her pregnancies;

Every man who accepts responsibility for his own and his family's well-being;

Every older person who protected their health while they were younger;

Everyone who avoids health risks with better information and responsible behaviour;

Everyone who has choices and control over the key decisions in their lives.

Since 1969, countries in Asia, Africa and Latin America have improved health care and education, and made them available to a wider population.

One result is that in most countries women and men want fewer children and **families are smaller** than in earlier generations; more newborns are surviving the risky first year of life, and older people are living longer than ever before.

In developing countries, **fertility has fallen by half since 1969,** from almost six children per woman to under three. As a result, **population growth has begun to slow.**

On the negative side, the **poorest countries often have the highest population growth rates. In 62 countries in Africa, Asia and Latin America, over 40 per cent of the population is under age 15. The poorest countries also have the worst reproductive health,** the highest rates of maternal mortality and the lowest rates of family planning use — often under 15 per cent, a level the average developing country had already reached by 1969.

Since 1969, when UNFPA (the United Nations Fund for Population Activities, later renamed the United Nations Population Fund) began operations, population has grown from 3.7 billion to 6 billion. But annual rates of population growth have slowed from 2.04 to 1.33 per cent, and should fall further. Annual additions peaked in 1985-1990 at 86 million. They should fall gradually in the next 20 years and more rapidly thereafter.

This slowing of population growth is not inevitable. The work of many

Continued slowing of population growth is not inevitable. It will depend on choices and actions in the next 10 years.

people over the last 30 years made it possible. Whether it continues, and whether it is accompanied by increasing well-being or increasing stress, will depend on choices and action in the next 10 years.

It will depend on the success of population and development policies, and in particular on universal exercise of the right to health including reproductive health.

We are still far from achieving this goal.

For example:

- More than half of the days of healthy life that women lose in their reproductive years are related to pregnancy, complications of pregnancy and reproductive disorders[1];

- 350 million women — nearly one third of all women of reproductive age in developing countries — still do not have access to a range of modern, safe and acceptable methods of family planning; 120 million more women would use family planning now if it were more widely available, better understood, supported by communities and families, and backed by quality programmes;

- 585,000 women in developing countries die every year as a result of pregnancy, and many times that number of women suffer infection or injury;

- 70,000 lives are lost each year to unsafe abortions;

BOX 1

1

Population May Grow to 8.9 Billion by 2050

The Population Division of the United Nations Department of Economic and Social Affairs projects that world population will grow from 6 billion in 1999 to between 7.3 and 10.7 billion by 2050, with 8.9 billion considered most likely. The 3.4 billion difference between the high and low projections, which reflect varying assumptions about future fertility rates, is as much as the total world population in 1966.

The current growth rate is 1.33 per cent. In the median projection, annual increments are expected to decline gradually from 78 million today to 64 million in 2020-2025, and then sharply to 33 million in 2045-2050.

FIGURE 1: World Population Growth, Actual and Projected, 1950-2050

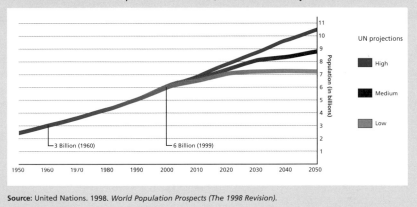

Source: United Nations. 1998. *World Population Prospects (The 1998 Revision).*

- Women are nearly two thirds of the world's 960 million illiterates, and women and girls make up three fifths of the world's poor;

- Violence against women is endemic in all countries, and many countries lack legal sanctions, or power to enforce them. As many as half of all women may be subject to gender-based violence at some point in their lives. Each year, 2 million girls and women are at risk of female genital mutilation (FGM);

- HIV/AIDS is shortening lifespans in the worst-affected countries; women are more vulnerable than men to HIV infection; half of new infections are to young people;

- International assistance for development has fallen from a peak of around $61 billion in 1992 to just over $48 billion in 1997. While population assistance is taking a larger share of donor funds (3.1 per cent compared with about 1.3 per cent), it is a bigger slice of a smaller pie, and still far short of agreed goals.

Poverty is not confined to the poorest countries. Over a billion people are still deprived of basic needs. Of the 4.8 billion people in developing countries, nearly three fifths lack basic sanitation.

Almost a third have no access to clean water. A quarter do not have adequate housing. A fifth have no access to modern health services. A fifth of children do not attend school to grade 5. About a fifth do not have enough dietary energy and protein. Micronutrient deficiencies are even more widespread. Worldwide, 2 billion people are anaemic, including 55 million in industrial countries.[2]

The poor are most exposed to fumes and polluted rivers and least able to protect themselves. Of the estimated 2.7 million deaths each year from air pollution, 2.2 million are from indoor pollution, and 80 per cent of the victims are rural poor in developing countries.

Needs for the future

For the future, food security will be critical. For example, to feed a population of 8.9 billion adequately would require nearly twice the basic calories consumed today. Access to water will also be critical.

Evidence has accumulated since world population passed 5 billion in 1987 that wasteful and unbalanced consumption patterns together with growing human numbers have profoundly affected the global climate. The United Nations Conference on Environment and Development in 1992 acknowledged that demographic factors, along with income levels, production technologies and consumption patterns, influence environmental outcomes. Gradual warming of the earth's atmosphere is a fact; the question remains what effect it will have. Large-scale global climate change could occur very rapidly if adverse trends reinforce each other.[3]

There is no sign of a global 'birth dearth'.

Possible changes, such as a rise in sea level, increased rainfall in some places or higher temperatures in others, will affect billions of people. For example, a rise of 50 centimetres in sea level would inundate 11 out of 13 of the world's major cities. More than half (3.2 billion) of the world's people live within 200 kilometres of a sea coast.

The growing number of poor people in poor countries is a rebuke to everyone concerned for social justice, the environment and development. Governments and the international community must acknowledge their responsibility to end extreme poverty. Rapid population growth is only one among many concerns, but it contributes to environmental damage, pressure on land and water resources, and political instability.

The cumulative effects of continuing poverty, malnutrition and ill health on a massive scale; gender discrimination and inequities in key areas such as education and health, including reproductive health; new threats such as HIV/ AIDS; environmental change; and shrinking international resources for development have the potential to wipe out the benefits of lower fertility over the past generation, with global consequences.

Demographic Trends

More than in any year since UNFPA started work in 1969, demographic trends are diverse and diverging.

High fertility: Population is growing fastest in the poorest countries, those least able to provide for basic needs and

BOX 2

1

Longer Lives + Falling Birth Rates = Slower Population Growth

Longer lives mean more people. How will that help to slow population growth?
Better health and longer lifespans encourage the idea that life is an investment, not a lottery. Experience shows that when people have the choice, they choose smaller families than previous generations did. When more people can decide how many children to have, the result is smaller but healthier families, and eventually longer lives and slower population growth.

If families are smaller, why is population still growing?
Fertility and birth rates have been falling in many countries for a long time. Smaller families mean lower population growth rates and in the long run smaller annual additions to world population. Women in developing countries are having half as many children as their counterparts in 1969.

But there are nearly twice as many women of childbearing age today. Together with better child survival and extended lifespans, this has kept annual additions to world population around 80 million a year for the last decade. Annual births will continue near current levels for much of the next 20 years.

---

create opportunities. Within countries, the poorest families also tend to be the largest ones, but poverty of choices may be as important as poverty of means in determining family size. The people and countries most affected are concentrated in Africa and South Asia, but there are some in every developing region.

The fastest-growing regions of the world are sub-Saharan Africa, parts of South Asia and West Asia. Their share of the global population has been increasing steadily for 40 years. These regions are joining other regions in becoming predominantly urban.

Low fertility: At the same time, 61 countries are seeing fertility at or below replacement level, and their populations could decline over the long term. As fertility falls in more countries, this phenomenon could affect countries with as many as two thirds of the world's people. There is no sign of a global "birth dearth", however: births will continue at over 100 million a year for the next 50 years. Deaths will rise during this period as populations become increasingly older.

This slow demographic change calls for policy choices: there will be implications for the structure of health care, pensions and social security, and for family relationships and inter-generational responsibility. Low-fertility countries will look to active older people and immigrants to supply some needed services and contribute to the economy.

One apparent choice, higher birth rates and larger families, is not open to low-fertility countries. No country in history has ever succeeded in raising birth rates over a long period once they have started to decline.

Rising death rates and shorter lifespans: In the countries most affected by HIV/AIDS, death rates are rising and life expectancy is falling fast enough to wipe out the gains of the last 20 years. The published figures are estimates and may well understate the full impact of the pandemic. Many countries are still unwilling to acknowledge how seriously they are affected, but in the absence of firm and immediate action to control the spread of the infection, all the evidence points to a greater catastrophe. Many of the worst-affected countries are among the poorest in the world and will depend heavily on outside help to combat the disease.

Population movements: Fluctuations in population growth and location are features of many countries affected by internal instability, natural disasters and social disruption. Some countries have experienced a rapid population influx, others a loss through out-migration, notably in the former Soviet republics of Central Asia. This population loss is probably a short-term phenomenon, but it raises policy questions — for example, about replacing the skills of migrants.

An estimated 13 million refugees have fled their own countries to escape from persecution, armed conflict or violence. An unknown but considerable number have been forced to leave for social or environmental reasons but do not qualify as refugees. Tens of millions are displaced within their own countries, many swelling the numbers of the urban poor.[4]

In all regions, international migration is moving nearer to the top of the policy agenda as the numbers of migrants increase and the issues they raise become more urgent. Only 2 per cent of the world's population are migrants. However, their impact on both sending and receiving countries is out of proportion to their numbers. Migrants send more than $70 billion to their home countries each year in the form of remittances, and industries in some host countries depend on the labour and skills of foreign-born workers.

The number of countries contributing to international migration streams has also increased in recent decades.

Migration within countries also dramatically affects the prospects for national development and the life condition of millions. Urban growth is fuelled both by natural population growth in cities and by rural-to-urban migration. In many countries and regions, urban-to-urban migration and rural-to-rural migration have become significant. These flows respond to and further contribute to stress on the environment and on service delivery systems. Older and poorer populations, and particularly older women, are further marginalized by increased migration from their communities.

ICPD: An Agenda for Choices

Today's new generation of young people bears both the burdens and the consequences of choice. They will decide how fast the world adds the next billion and the billion after that, and whether world population doubles again. Their decisions will influence whether the new billions will be born to lives of poverty and deprivation; whether equality and equity will be established between women and men; and what effect population growth will have on natural resources and the global environment. These are personal decisions, but they will be influenced by the policy choices of nations and the global community.

BOX 3

Goals of the ICPD — and New Benchmarks

The ICPD endorsed a set of interdependent population and development objectives, including sustained economic growth in the context of sustainable development, and gender equity and equality. Countries were urged to include population factors in all development strategies, and to act to eliminate gender-based violence and harmful traditional practices including female genital mutilation. Quantitative goals were adopted in three areas:

- **Universal education** — Elimination of the gender gap in primary and secondary education by 2005, and complete access to primary school or the equivalent by both girls and boys as quickly as possible and in any case before 2015;

- **Mortality reduction** — Reduction in infant and under-5 mortality rates by at least one third, to no more than 50 and 70 per 1,000 live births, respectively, by 2000, and to below 35 and 45, respectively, by 2015; reduction in maternal mortality to half the 1990 levels by 2000 and by a further one half by 2015 (specifically, in countries with the highest levels of mortality, to below 60 per 100,000 live births);

- **Reproductive health** — Provision of universal access to a full range of safe and reliable family-planning methods and to related reproductive and sexual health services by 2015.

The five-year review in 1999 agreed on new benchmarks to measure implementation of ICPD goals:

- The 1990 illiteracy rate for women and girls should be halved by 2005. By 2010 the net primary school enrolment ratio for children of both sexes should be at least 90 per cent;

- By 2005, 60 per cent of primary health care and family planning facilities should offer the widest achievable range of safe and effective family planning methods, essential obstetric care, prevention and management of reproductive tract infections including STDs, and barrier methods to prevent infection; 80 per cent of facilities should offer such services by 2010, and all should do so by 2015;

- At least 40 per cent of all births should be assisted by skilled attendants where the maternal mortality rate is very high, and 80 per cent globally, by 2005; these figures should be 50 and 85 per cent, respectively, by 2010; and 60 and 90 per cent by 2015;

- Any gap between the proportion of individuals using contraceptives and the proportion expressing a desire to space or limit their families should be reduced by half by 2005, 75 per cent by 2010, and 100 per cent by 2015. Recruitment targets or quotas should not be used in attempting to reach this goal.

Recognizing that the HIV/AIDS situation is worse than anticipated by the ICPD, the review agreed that to reduce vulnerability to HIV/AIDS infection, at least 90 per cent of young men and women aged 15 to 24 should have access by 2005 to preventive methods — such as female and male condoms, voluntary testing, counselling, and follow-up — and at least 95 per cent by 2010. HIV infection rates in persons 15 to 24 years of age should be reduced by 25 per cent in the most-affected countries by 2005, and by 25 per cent globally by 2010.

Source: United Nations. 1999. *Report of the Ad Hoc Committee of the Whole of the Twenty-first Special Session of the General Assembly* (A/S-21/5/Add.1).

Despite demographic uncertainty, faltering development in many countries and the decline in international resources for development, the climate for choice is better in two crucial ways than it was when the world passed 5 billion:

- Countries have reached a broad global consensus on population and development, and agreed on an agenda for implementing it. The agenda is based on the understanding that each sovereign country will implement the agenda according to its own priorities and perceptions; that reaching slower and more-balanced population growth worldwide depends on the free and informed choices of individual men and women; and that women and men must be empowered to make those choices;

> *More and more countries are measuring the success of reproductive health services by their ability to satisfy people's needs, rather than by their effect on fertility levels.*

- There is growing practical evidence that this agenda meets the needs of people and nations and that despite all obstacles, it is being put into practice.

At the 1994 International Conference on Population and Development (ICPD) in Cairo, 179 countries reached consensus on the relationship between population and development, and set goals for 2015. A five-year review in 1999 has shown that the goals of ICPD remain not only practical and realistic, but also necessary for individual advancement and balanced development.

The ICPD recognized, and the review confirmed and strengthened, that countries are adopting population and development policies based on quality of life, personal choice and human rights. Policies are concerned with such issues as poverty, food security, resource use and environmental impacts; data on population numbers, distribution and rates of growth are used to promote broad development rather than narrow sectoral goals.

In this growing group of countries the success of reproductive health and related services is measured by their ability to satisfy human needs and aspirations rather than by their effect on fertility levels. Among the primary concerns are attention to ensuring informed choice, access for poor and rural populations, and uniform high quality.

The Cairo conference also recognized that meeting reproductive health needs involves providing a range of services, including family planning, and at the same time taking action to guarantee rights, inform and empower women in all aspects of their lives, and involve men as supportive partners. It is central to the ICPD consensus that fertility is determined by the voluntary decisions of couples and individuals. There is a clear understanding that smaller families and slower population growth overall will be the result of policies enabling everyone, but especially women, to exercise choices in all areas of their lives.

Countries are changing the legal framework and implementing existing legislation in pursuit of these goals. There is also an increasing emphasis on advocacy and on partnerships between government and civil society to build support for the goals of ICPD.

There is agreement on the resources needed, though countries and the international community have not yet made good on the agreement.

Many countries have made considerable progress towards the goals agreed at the ICPD. All countries have taken some steps and many would do more if the necessary resources were available. At the same time there is pressure from many groups, especially those representing women and young people, for faster and more focused action to make the promise of ICPD a reality.

The "ICPD+5" year of 1999 was the occasion to review implementation of the Programme of Action and consider action for the future. UNFPA, the United Nations Population Division and various non-governmental organizations (NGOs) conducted surveys, and UNFPA organized a series of expert meetings leading up to an international forum at The Hague in February 1999. Finally, the United Nations General Assembly held a special session on the ICPD from 30 June to 2 July 1999.

The Hague Forum and the General Assembly special session were occasions for governments, parliamentarians, NGOs and private donors to share their experiences and understandings. They assessed progress towards the goals of the Programme of Action, considered emerging issues such as migration and ageing, defined new benchmarks to measure implementation, and made recommendations to adapt activities to evolving circumstances.

Actions were agreed upon in several categories: population and development;

reproductive and sexual health; gender equality, equity and the empowerment of women; partnerships and collaboration; and mobilization of resources.

Population and Development

In the five years since the ICPD, countries have adopted new policies or adapted old ones, intensified policy discussion, and opened dialogue in new areas.

- Nearly half of all countries have reviewed their policies in light of the new understandings of the role of population in development;

- More than one third have updated their population policies to be consistent with ICPD objectives or have integrated factors relating to healthcare quality, gender equality and equity, and improvement of information systems into long-term development plans;

- Two thirds of all countries have introduced policy or legislative measures to promote gender equity and equality and the empowerment of women, including in the areas of inheritance, property rights and employment, and in protection from gender-based violence.

Additionally, programme strategies and operating procedures have changed. New monitoring mechanisms and better means of collecting and using data have been put in place. Organizations of lawmakers; women; youth; traditional leaders; cultural, health and other advocates; and policy makers are involved in population and development.

Growing democracy, expanded participation in voluntary associations and improvements in communications have encouraged the participatory approach at the centre of the ICPD Programme of Action. The devolution of public responsibilities, decentralization of public administrations and other institutional changes have also greatly accelerated and changed the context of population and development activities.

Chronic high rates of population growth narrow countries' development options, because available resources must go towards essential services. Slower population growth offers developing countries an opportunity to strengthen social, economic and political structures. Fewer births and more working-age people increase the potential for improving health and education, investing in human skills, accelerated wealth creation and increased social participation.

People who have fewer children invest more in their health and education.

This has been the pattern in East and South-east Asia and in many developing countries elsewhere. The combined effect of lower fertility and mortality is a rapid increase in the proportion of the population in working ages. This shift helps increase household and national savings and investment, and particularly social expenditures.[5]

But development is not a smooth process. The financial crisis that began in South-east Asia in 1997 has thrown millions into poverty and deep distress, which in some countries has been compounded by the absence of social cohesion and dependable political institutions. A UNFPA study[6] indicates that the crisis and resulting cuts in social programmes have had a severe social impact, particularly on women's rights and reproductive health (see page 17).

The changes in social policy which developing countries have made in response to the fresh consensus on population and development call for comparable changes in international economic structures, to reinforce rather than weaken the consensus.

So far, however, the changes in perceptions of population and development have not been matched by economic changes. Global and private consumption reached $24 trillion in 1998, more than twice what it was in UNFPA's early years, and the wealthiest groups and individuals control a larger share of it than ever. The wealthiest fifth of the world's people consume more than 66 times the materials and resources of the poorest fifth. Economic development raises prices as well as incomes. The last to benefit are the poorest, who spend more of their incomes on essentials such as food and housing and depend most on public services, especially health, education and transport.

The ICPD agreed that population is integrally related to development. The five-year review recommended that governments should:

- Look for better understanding of the relationships among population, poverty, gender inequity and inequality, health, education, the environment, financial and human resources, and development;

- Re-examine recent research concerning the relationships among reductions in fertility and economic growth and its equitable distribution;

• Draw attention to and promote linkages among macroeconomic, environmental and social policies.

Social investment, demographic change and development

Important choices must be made regarding investments in education, particularly of girls and women, and in health, including reproductive health and mortality reduction. Decisions to invest in these areas can initiate dramatic changes in reproductive behaviour, and will shape the demographic future.

Declines in fertility and mortality are mutually reinforcing. Fertility decline is often associated with postponing the first birth, waiting longer intervals between births and having fewer children late in reproductive life.

People who have fewer children invest more in their children's health and education.[7] This raises the perceived costs of children but also raises the perceived benefits to the parents from fewer but better prepared offspring.

Women who have been to school understand that proper care for children includes support for their education. The more education women have, the more education their children are likely to have. Educated mothers are more likely to invest in the health of their children and use information and services to protect their children's health.

Mortality increases in some countries

In a number of countries in Eastern Europe and the former Soviet Union, adult mortality has increased as the re-sult of growing poverty, poor nutrition, increased stress and overcrowding, infectious diseases and deteriorating health care across the board.

The deadliest factor affecting demographic change in the short term, however, is HIV/AIDS. In several sub-Saharan African countries, the epidemic has slashed population growth rates, at an enormous and tragic cost to families and communities.

Reproductive and Sexual Health and Rights

The five-year review of ICPD recognized the importance of the right to health, including reproductive health, in health-sector reform and made recommendations on programme priorities in family planning, maternal health, prevention of sexually transmitted diseases (STDs) including HIV/AIDS, and adolescent reproductive health. It urged governments to, among other things:

• Increase skilled attendance in childbirth;

• Review laws affecting reproductive health;

• Increase investments to improve the quality and availability of sexual and reproductive health services, including voluntary, quality family planning;

• Involve communities, non-governmental organizations and the private sector in designing, implementing, monitoring and evaluating programmes;

• Promote male responsibility for protecting their own and their partners' sexual and reproductive health, preventing unwanted pregnancy and the spread of sexually transmitted diseases, sharing household and child-rearing responsibilities, and helping eliminate harmful practices, coercion and sexual violence;

- Ensure availability of reproductive health information, services and products, including contraceptives, to allow all couples and individuals to exercise their right to decide the number, spacing and timing of their children and to have the information and means to do so;

- Recognize the connection between maternal mortality and poverty, and work to reduce maternal mortality and morbidity as a public health priority;

- Ensure that women have ready access to essential obstetric care, adequate maternal health-care services, skilled attendance at delivery, emergency obstetric care, referral and transport to higher levels of care when necessary, post-partum care and family planning;

- Provide education and services — including voluntary HIV testing and counselling, and access to female and male condoms — to prevent the transmission of sexually transmitted diseases and HIV, as an integral part of primary health care;

- Mobilize society to address the social and economic factors contributing to

HIV risk and vulnerability, and promote responsible sexual behaviour based on mutual respect and gender equity in sexual relationships;

- Prevent sexual exploitation of young women and children;

- Ensure that refugees and people in emergency situations receive sexual and reproductive health care and information, and greater protection from sexual and gender-based violence;

- Eliminate harmful traditional practices, such as female genital mutilation;

- Work with parents, communities, schools and youth to ensure that adolescents have appropriate information, assistance and services for responsible and healthy sexual and reproductive behaviour.

Broader choice, better quality

In keeping with the needs-based approach to reproductive health agreed to at the ICPD, the focus of programmes and policies is shifting from service providers to their clients, though not at the same speed in all countries. In successful programmes, results are increasingly being measured by the quality of service and the responsiveness and expertise of service providers.

But it is harder to measure quality than count heads, so a lot of work since the ICPD has gone into finding reliable ways to assess programme performance based on the new criteria, for example

> *Providing better information and counselling, and involving communities, leads to greater client satisfaction and increased demand for services.*

by establishing participatory planning, monitoring and evaluation. Lessons learned are starting to be translated into regular cycles of planning, action and review, resulting in continuous improvement. This process is reinforced by training and retraining service providers and securing their commitment to quality service delivery.

Experience in Nepal, the Philippines, Ghana, Kenya and other countries shows that with proper staff training the proportion of clients receiving higher-quality information and counselling can be dramatically increased within a short time, and that community participation amplifies the benefits. Responsive and client-centred programmes, backed by sufficient funding and managerial support, and including attention to multiple health concerns, increase clients' satisfaction and raise their expectations. This draws more clients into the system, further increasing demand for integrated services. Quality of service affects clients' choices and encourages health-promoting behaviours.[8]

These efforts accelerate national programmes' ability to adjust and adapt to changing circumstances and improve their responsiveness and accountability to the people they serve. They bring out the best efforts of governments, the private sector, and social, voluntary and community-based organizations.

Obstacles

Not all of the reproductive health concerns set out in the Programme of Action however, have called forth the required response:

- It has been hard to secure the necessary resources or policy priority to reduce maternal mortality, despite well-known and widely available techniques, and despite universal agreement that it should be a programme priority. One study found that where maternal mortality is very high — more than one death in every 100 pregnant women — the risk could be reduced by as much as 80 per cent by providing antenatal care, information about warning signs and services to provide emergency care.[9]

- Providing appropriate information and services for unmarried adolescents and young adults has been difficult in many countries.

- The HIV/AIDS pandemic has advanced faster than projected in 1994 at the time of the ICPD.

Maternal mortality

Reducing maternal mortality and morbidity has been a goal of government policies and programmes since the Safe Motherhood Initiative was launched in 1987, but there has been little or no progress. A systematic effort to reduce the overall risk of maternity calls for a range of interventions, including: skilled help during and after delivery; emergency referral and obstetric care, expanded information and education about health, pregnancy and childbirth, pre- and post-natal care; improved nutrition; and greater access by women to resources, information and the power to make their own decisions. The ICPD review agreed on new benchmarks for reducing maternal mortality.

The youth debate

There are currently over 1 billion young people between the ages of 15 and 24,

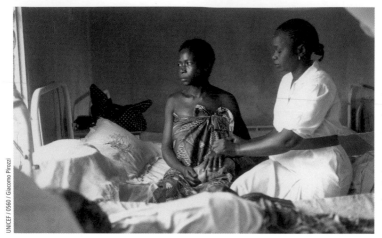

There has been litt[
progress in reducir
the risk of child-
birth. Left, nurse ir
Sierra Leone mater
nity ward examine
patient who had n
prenatal care and
whose child was
stillborn. Sierra
Leone has one of
the world's highest
maternal mortality
rates, 1,800 deaths
per 100,000 births.

the largest number ever. Many are married, though fewer proportionately than a generation ago; more are sexually active. Today's young people are frequently at risk — of unwanted pregnancy, HIV/AIDS and other sexually transmitted diseases, sexual exploitation, and alienation from parents and communities. A key concern is the growing number of young people living outside families or in disrupted family situations.

How best to meet young people's reproductive health needs is a matter for discussion and national decision. It has often proved difficult to reconcile the important role of parents with the capacity of young people to make their own decisions as they grow towards adulthood, or to define the role of society in mediating what is primarily a family matter.

Ignoring the issue, however, incurs a high cost in ill health, wasted life opportunities and social disruption. There is strong evidence that offering informed choices to the young reinforces responsibility and encourages responsible adulthood and parenthood. On this basis, many countries are designing policies and programmes for youth, including reproductive health; and recognition is growing that the involvement of young people themselves in preparing and putting these programmes into action is essential to their success.[10] Some programmes successfully involve older family members and the community in advising and informing young people.

The ICPD agreed that young people have the same right to reproductive health as their elders, though it is acknowledged that the right to reproductive health is a sensitive issue as it regards youth; societies will have different approaches and will come to different conclusions about how to achieve the goal of adolescent reproductive health.

HIV/AIDS

New infections now number 11 a minute, and over half of those infected are young people below the age of 24. Other sexually transmitted diseases are also disproportionately found in younger men and women; an untreated sexually transmitted disease increases the risk of HIV infection tenfold.

Young women are particularly at risk because of biological susceptibility, their vulnerability to unwanted and coerced sex and their inability to negotiate safe sex.

Within groups engaging in high-risk behaviours, HIV prevalence can increase from under 5 per cent to over 50 per cent within one or two years.[11] From these groups (for example prostitutes and their clients, others with multiple unprotected sex partners, and needle-sharing drug users) the virus passes readily through social networks and contaminated blood supplies to the general population.

Strong prevention programmes can avert an even more devastating catastrophe. Some affected countries have been very successful in reducing the incidence of new HIV/AIDS infections in young populations. In Uganda and Thailand the incidence of new infections, particularly in young populations, has declined by about one third in response to intensive information and protection campaigns. Among adolescents, in particular, prevalence levels have reversed among young women appearing for prenatal care.

Gender Equality and Women's Empowerment

The ICPD review called on countries to promote and protect the human rights of women and girls, with policies including zero tolerance of violence against girls and women and promotion of male responsibility.

UNFPA's 30 years have seen remarkable progress in women's collective status and individual prospects. The ICPD Programme of Action and the Platform for Action adopted by the Fourth World Conference on Women in Beijing in 1995 reflected decades of effort by and on behalf of women.

The advances, while incomplete, include:

BOX 4

Countering Violence and Coercion Directed at Women

Since the ICPD and the Beijing Conference, thanks to the efforts of women's NGOs around the world, there is growing appreciation that violence and threats of violence pervade women's lives, and contribute greatly to the denial of women's human rights, including their right to reproductive health.

The March 1999 session of the Commission on the Status of Women examined gender violence in its various forms.

The Commission adopted and is submitting to the General Assembly an Optional Protocol to the Convention on the Elimination of All Forms of Discrimination against Women. It establishes procedures for individuals or groups to submit documented claims of rights violations to the Committee on the Elimination of Discrimination against Women, once domestic remedies are exhausted, unreasonably prolonged or unlikely to bring relief. The Protocol would also enable the Committee to initiate investigations into grave or systematic violations of women's rights in countries that have agreed to accept the inquiry procedure.

- Improvements in educational enrolment and literacy;

- Increased participation in the paid labour force;

- Increased participation in management and administration;

- Greater use of the voting franchise and attainment of political representation;

- Legal action to establish and protect women's rights in marriage, inheritance and property;

- Greater access to and control over resources through employment and micro-credit programmes;

- Recognition that gender-based violence is a social not a family matter. Many countries have revised laws and family codes to strengthen measures against female genital mutilation, rape, forced marriage, domestic violence, dowry murder, and "honour" killings. For example, 15 African countries have outlawed FGM;

- Stronger mechanisms for addressing women's rights issues as basic human rights concerns.

Progress in reproductive health since 1969 has directly contributed to women's empowerment. The ability to make informed choices about the number, timing and spacing of children accommodates women's need for education, which is often interrupted by early pregnancy or marriage; improves maternal and child health; and encourages balanced consideration of employment and family opportunities. This in turn increases the scope for practical choice and promotes healthier families.

Many important advances since the ICPD have been made as the result of the growing strength of women's organizations at all levels, and their increasing ability to forge productive alliances with governments, as well as with legislators and other civil-society actors, on the basis of the ICPD consensus. Working together, these alliances have been able to secure legislative change and action to back it up, to change administration and increasingly to change underlying attitudes towards gender issues.

Much remains to be done to address both new threats and persistent problems. The HIV/AIDS pandemic is much worse than was anticipated in 1994. Increases in awareness, participation, organization and action have not yet reversed the continuing feminization of poverty[12] or reduced maternal mortality and morbidity.

Further action is needed to:

- Enable women to avoid unwanted sex, pregnancy, and sexually transmitted diseases, including HIV/AIDS;

- Reduce the persistence of male sexual aggression and the values that support it;

- Improve communication about sexual and reproductive concerns between spouses or with their children;

- Appropriately value women's contributions to their families and societies;

- Increase women's opportunities for social and economic participation;

- Increase male participation in the family and the household;

- Enable men to share expectations and responsibilities and reduce the frustrations that contribute to gender violence.

Men's roles

The need to involve men in advancing women's reproductive rights and health, and also to ensure the reproductive health of men, has raised fundamental questions about programme design and orientation. Reaching agreement on how to approach these issues has proved difficult.

Women are more at risk than men from sexually transmitted diseases and other health hazards; but in many societies decisions affecting sexual health are reserved for men. Men need to appreciate the risks and lost opportunities entailed in gender inequality. They must learn to support women's social and reproductive rights, and closer partnerships to achieve them.

Programmes need to encourage men to undertake actions: in support of women's rights and empowerment in family and public settings; in the socialization of male children; in improving women's health; and in eradicating gender violence and sexual exploitation.

Partnerships and Participation

The five-year review of ICPD has referred at all points to the importance of partnership in reaching its goals.

Governments were responsible for the ICPD consensus, but parliamentarians, the private sector, and non-governmental organizations played an important part. NGOs and civil-society groups involved in the review process included development agencies, women's groups, health and youth advocates, religious groups, professional associations, indigenous people's organizations, and community groups.

As countries have moved to implement the ICPD Programme of Action, the involvement of civil society has increased. More than 40 countries have formal mechanisms to bring NGOs into policy discussions, and many more have informal mechanisms.[13]

Some concerns remain. Many NGOs are relatively small, under-financed and dependent on external technical and financial resources, and there are sometimes doubts about whose interests they represent. NGOs may raise awkward questions which may be interpreted as attacks on national development policy rather than constructive criticism.

These are legitimate concerns, but the review recognized that they should be confronted and mechanisms established for cooperation among government officials, private-sector representatives and other civil-society organizations. The comparative advantages and potential of different organizations need to be better explored and utilized. Civil-society organizations are a valuable resource for mobilizing national efforts to advocate for and implement the Programme of Action.

Involvement of NGOs and the private sector is particularly important because of the changing role of governments as providers of basic social services. A growing number of countries are adopting decentralized management and decision-making. The involvement of grass-roots organizations will be essential to provide a voice, information and services to communities, and to people — the poor, the unmarried, and young people without parents, for example — who might otherwise be marginalized or forgotten. NGOs also do valuable work in providing assistance in times of crisis or disaster, supplying the needs and representing the interests of the victims.

More than 40 countries now have formal mechanisms to bring NGOs into policy discussions.

Governments need to make a positive decision to engage communities and their representatives in discussion about population and development issues. This choice can preserve and protect the valuable aspects of tradition and culture while jettisoning harmful and risky practices. The positive results of dialogue and collaboration can be seen in the progress made by the Sabiny Elders Association in the Kapchorwa district of Uganda in replacing female genital mutilation with a ceremony welcoming young girls into the society as adults.[14]

Improvements in participation and information stimulate each other. The cost of making information available can be low with a balanced plan of mass media and more local communication. When information and communication are designed to generate behaviour change as well as raise awareness, they can stimulate demand for quality and accountability in service delivery.[15]

Reaching the goals of the ICPD Programme of Action will require partnerships representing a wide range of interests, perspectives and development aims, including reproductive health and rights. Civil society has a part to play in policy formulation and programme implementation. Its groups address diverse concerns and their range of experience and interests can encourage progress in relatively neglected areas such as addressing gender violence, ensuring reproductive rights, adapting societies to changing age structures, changing unsustainable patterns of resource use, coping with migration and promoting gender equality. Civic groups with an interest in different issues share a common interest in accelerating social and economic development and need responsive public institutions to be most effective.

The Question of Resources

Partnership has an international dimension. Cooperation among industrial and developing countries is critical to the successful implementation of ICPD.

The ICPD Programme of Action spelled out the resources needed for a basic package of reproductive health and population programmes. It also indicated where investment was needed to empower women, reduce mortality and morbidity, and provide basic education (particularly of girls and women).

The financial constraints on the implementation of the Programme of Action are severe and have worsened over time. Developing countries and countries with economies in transition have had difficulty finding the necessary resources from their own budgets, and development cooperation has also fallen short. A few developed countries — including Denmark, the Netherlands, Norway and Sweden — are meeting the internationally agreed target level for development assistance of 0.7 per cent of gross national product; others like the United Kingdom have promised to do so. But some of the biggest donor countries — including Germany and the United States — remain far below the target.

Governments negotiated specific agreements at the ICPD, including estimates of the levels of national and international resources required to implement the consensus. They now face critical decisions about whether they will commit the necessary resources to realize their vision. It was estimated that $17 billion would be required annually by the year 2000 for the successful implementation of a basic integrated package of population and reproductive health activities. It was further estimated that about one third ($5.7 billion) of the resources would be supplied to countries through external assistance and about two thirds ($11.3 billion) would be mobilized within the countries themselves.

As of 1997, industrial countries had reached $1.9-2.0 billion, and developing countries about $7.7 billion. There was no expectation of improvement in 1998, implying that the goal for the year 2000 would be missed by a wide margin.

In human terms, these shortfalls imply that women will continue to endure unwanted pregnancy, or resort to abortion; that they will continue to die as a result of their pregnancy; that their children will still be at risk; that HIV/AIDS will continue its rapid spread; and that progress towards human rights and equality in health care will be slower than ever.

While development assistance from industrial countries has fallen, emer-

International assistance for population and reproductive health is far short of developing countries' needs.

gency needs and allocations to disaster relief and peace-keeping missions have rapidly increased. It is clear to all that effective development assistance will prevent many disasters and emergencies, and that the long-term cost will be lower. But despite all urging and the commitment of many countries, the will to move from perception to action has not yet seized the biggest donors.

At the same time, private-sector institutions and foundations in donor countries, especially the United States, are playing a larger role. The United Nations Foundation for International Partnership, the Packard Foundation and others have committed over $500 million to support projects during the next five years. Over $7 billion has been added to the William H. Gates Foundation endowment to support a range of health and development initiatives. These new sources of assistance make important contributions in specific areas, but they are not a substitute for national commitment to international development.

It was fundamental to the consensus of ICPD that well-managed investments in long-term development help to build the capacity to manage development and encourage self-reliance, forestalling the conditions that lead to national instability and insecurity.[16]

Expanding the level and variety of committed resources and better managing their use is an urgent priority. New efforts for better coordination among donors and with governments and civil-society institutions show promise; these include South-South cooperation, the

20/20 Initiative, and the Asia Initiative undertaken by the European Union in cooperation with UNFPA (see Chapter 4).

Going Forward

This year's *State of World Population* report reviews experience in the first four years of implementation of the 20-year ICPD Programme of Action, including the major conclusions of the international reviews undertaken in 1999: the Hague Forum and the special session of the United Nations General Assembly.

The first conclusion is one of considerable growth in the efforts to implement the Programme of Action. Despite severe resource constraints, the five-year review of implementation experience has shown that an approach to development centred on individual needs and aspirations can create integrated programmes for sexual and reproductive health, advance the empowerment of women and mobilize new partnerships among governments and civil society.

The technical meetings, round tables, regional conferences and intergovernmental meetings of the past year, and dozens of other inquiries and studies undertaken by governments, international organizations and non-governmental organizations have amply documented the range of progress. They have made recommendations concerning the key areas for further progress in the next stages of implementation. Some actions have been easier than others, and progress has been influenced by local and institutional contexts.

The five-year review of ICPD has clarified what is needed for further advance.

Developing countries need:

- Population and development policies which establish broad goals clearly linked with the resources to achieve them;

- Institutional structures capable of adapting to changing policies;

- A commitment to gender equity and equality, greater participation of women in policy and decision making roles, partnership with men and action to end gender-based violence;

- Rapid movement towards reproductive health service integration and better referral systems;

- More-responsive services, better accountability to the people for whom the services are designed, and intensified attention to staff training, retention and management;

- Determined action to halt the spread of AIDS;

- A commitment to provide quality reproductive health services and information to young people including unmarried women;

- More effective decentralization;

- Improvements in the quality and use of data;

- Closer collaboration between government and civil society.

Above every other need, however is the need to make good the commitment

BOX 5

UNFPA: Building the Consensus

When the United Nations Fund for Population Activities (UNFPA, later renamed the United Nations Population Fund) started operations in 1969, population in the United Nations system was a matter of demographic enquiry, under the United Nations Population Division. It was barely possible to discuss population activities at the international level. By 1966, only 26 developing countries had national family planning programmes or substantial government support for family planning, and only a small minority of people outside the richer countries knew anything about family planning.

Population growth was at what proved to be a historic peak of 2 per cent a year, 2.5 per cent in developing countries; and total fertility in developing countries was also at its highest level, about six children per woman. There was a great deal of doubt among experts in the field whether family planning could be successfully promoted in developing countries, or that family planning programmes would help to bring population growth rates down. There were few women's health programmes unconnected with childbirth or child health.

UNFPA began its work as it has continued ever since, with a process of dialogue. Finding that African countries, for example, were interested mainly in collecting population data and building up the expertise to analyse it, UNFPA supported the United Nations Census Programme in over 30 countries, helping 21 countries take a population census for the first time. Latin American countries were concerned with building demographic information into development planning, and UNFPA supported the regional centre for demographic research, CELADE. In Asia, where there was a great deal of official interest in family planning, UNFPA supported its integration in governments' mother and child health-care programmes, and encouraged innovative organizations like the national family planning associations. Many UNFPA-funded projects were carried out by its partners in the United Nations system, building expertise and understanding of population and development.

By the time of the World Population Conference in 1974, UNFPA had established its global presence, with $52 million in resources and programmes in 97 countries.

The Conference was the first of its kind at ministerial level, and the World Population Plan of Action agreed there was the first political consensus on action in population and development. UNFPA, under its first Executive Director, Rafael Salas, played an important part in this process, having established its position as a trusted partner in countries of all ideological positions.

UNFPA understood early on that women's rights and status were not only important in themselves but would be critical to the success of population and development policies and programmes. Under the first Chief of its Programme Division, Dr. Nafis Sadik, later Executive Director, women's organizations were welcomed as partners of UNFPA, and governments were urged to involve them in the development process.

UNFPA's partnerships with donor and developing countries helped to demonstrate that population was a "programmable" part of development strategy, and that population assistance could be effectively delivered without ideological connotations and in conformity with sovereign countries' priorities and values. These understandings have been critical in building today's global consensus.

to provide resources. Without this, efforts in developing countries will be slowed, and in many countries stalled completely. A heavy responsibility rests with the donor nations to fill the gap between developing countries' capabilities and their needs.

National programmes, projects and strategies are frequently experiencing difficulties in coordinating newly developed structures and newly emerging functions. With further progress these may prove to have been growing pains: the temporary side-effect of increasing strength. Further development, however, will depend on political commitment and financial resources, both national and international.

The ICPD+5 review marks the latest stage of a process started 30 years ago. During this time population has moved from a minority concern of demographers and statisticians to a global consensus embracing everyone involved with human development — from a matter primarily of numbers and growth rates

to including human rights in the area of reproductive health and gender equity.

The right to choose the size and spacing of the family and to have the information and the means to do so, first enunciated in 1968, is no longer exercised only by the privileged few but by more than half of all couples throughout the world. Universal and equal access by women and men to education and health care, including reproductive and sexual health care, is an acknowledged goal of national and international development policy, and is increasingly found in practice. Population policy based on human rights and human needs has become a practical and necessary part of development strategy.

UNFPA has been a leading partner in calling attention to new concerns, building consensus, and encouraging action at both national and international levels. The next phase, mobilizing the will and the resources to meet the goals of the ICPD Programme of Action, is the challenge of the next decade.

CHAPTER 2

Population Change and People's Choices

UNINCEF / 1029 / Betty Press

The 20th century has witnessed unprecedented changes in both population dynamics and the progress of human development. Life opportunities for many women and men around the world have expanded like never before in history. At the same time, much of humanity remains caught in a vicious cycle of poverty, ill health and inequality.

The coexistence of these divergent demographic and social trends makes this a crucial moment of decision about our future. We now have unique opportunities to ensure people's well-being and human rights on a global scale and reap tremendous economic and social benefits; we can seize these opportunities and break the cycle by acting decisively and providing the necessary resources.

The ICPD in 1994 articulated a comprehensive approach to population and development which addresses many of the fundamental challenges facing the human community — including poverty alleviation, provision of health care and education, and preservation of the environment. Its emphasis on gender equality and equity and on meeting individual needs, especially needs for reproductive health information and services, represents an important end in itself.

Photo: Rwandan mother and sons were reunited in 1994 after a six-month separation caused by civil war. Around the world, wars and other emergencies have displaced tens of millions of people.

Neither the conference nor the five-year review adopted quantitative goals for population growth, structure or distribution. At the same time, both affirmed that implementing the Programme of Action would contribute to an early stabilization of world population, which, in turn, would make an important contribution to achieving sustainable development.

Where we are today

- Global population has quadrupled in 100 years, a rate of increase unknown in previous history.

- Life expectancies are increasing in most countries. A child born today has a better chance than ever before of surviving infancy and living a long, healthy life.

- There are more young people (over 1 billion aged 15-24) than ever before, and many developing countries have an unprecedented share of the population in their working-age years. At the same time, there are more older people than ever before, and populations are steadily ageing.

- A growing majority of women and men have the information and means to make choices about the number and spacing of their children.

- Education has become more accessible, to women as well as men, and its importance more widely appreciated.

- Communication and travel have become easier, accelerating the flow of ideas and people within and between countries.

- Women are gaining increasing control over their life choices. In diverse cultural settings, women are demanding equality with men in social and economic participation, decision-making and control of resources.

- Environmental degradation and climate change, new diseases, social disruption and economic instability all threaten people's health, livelihoods and security, and are spreading more widely and quickly than ever before. Fortunately, so can opportunity, technology and social progress.

The challenge for the coming years is to accelerate social and economic development, expand women's and men's control over their lives, including their reproductive lives, and enable them to enjoy their basic human rights. Meeting these goals will both contribute to and be facilitated by the stabilization of population growth.

Population and Development: Changing Policies

When UNFPA was started in 1969, many countries lacked population policies. Many developing countries, and most least-developed ones, had never conducted a census. Lacking basic information, national development strategies rarely took into account the impacts of population growth, location, movements (within the country or across borders) and age structure.

As data became available, many governments realized their populations were growing faster than expected,

BOX 6

Population and Development: New Conclusions

Falling mortality and declining fertility are presenting most developing countries with a one-time window of opportunity in which a higher proportion of the population is of working age than ever before. Faster fertility declines open the window wider, but for a shorter time. Taking advantage of this "demographic bonus" to advance economic development will require wide access to education and health (particularly reproductive and sexual health), information and services, and an end to discrimination against women in social participation and decision-making.

How declining mortality and fertility (and to a much smaller extent, larger populations and higher densities) can spur economic growth is becoming clearer, thanks to better data and methods of analysis. The poorest countries stand to gain the most from fertility and mortality declines if they can exploit the potential for growth.

Increased women's participation in the formal labour force, which often accompanies and reinforces fertility decline and greater educational opportunity, can also result in economic gains. Future income growth estimates need to take into account women's work at home and in the informal sector, as well as the now-uncounted costs of natural resource degradation.

Demographic and economic change also affects the proportion of people living in poverty. High fertility in poor countries increases poverty by retarding economic growth and skewing the distribution of income against the poor.

In the early stages of demographic transition, when mortality declines outpace fertility declines in poor households, income differentials between poor and non-poor households may increase. When poor families have fewer children, they have more resources to invest in their children or save, reducing poverty and inequality. In Brazil, 25 per cent of people born in 1970 are poor; it is estimated that 37 per cent would be poor if families in 1970 had been as large as those in 1900. Annual economic growth would have had to be 0.7 per cent higher in per capita gross domestic product to achieve an equivalent reduction in poverty without the lower fertility.

Evidence that high fertility exacerbates poverty justifies investments in reproductive health and voluntary family planning programmes as part of a broad social development strategy.

Source: Birdsall, Nancy, Allen C. Kelley and Steven Sinding (eds.). *Population Does Matter: Demography, Growth and Poverty in the Developing World* (forthcoming) Report of the Symposium on Population Change and Economic Development, a Conference sponsored by the Rockefeller Foundation, Packard Foundation and UNFPA, 2-6 November 1998, Bellagio, Italy.

hampering social and economic development. In every region, requests increased for assistance to improve the availability of information and services for family planning and maternal and child health. Policy development, research, institutional support, training and basic data collection continued to be important components of population assistance, but a growing share of investment was dedicated to service delivery.

Increased availability of family planning information and services met a growing demand for smaller and healthier families and spurred a near four-fold increase since 1969 in the proportion of couples using contraception. During the same period, access to basic health services also increased and in less-developed regions life expectancy at birth increased by over 10 years. Annual gross domestic product per capita

BOX 7

South-east Asian Crisis May Erase Development Progress

The South-east Asian economic crisis that began in 1997 provides a grim warning that global financial turmoil can wipe out developmental gains due to social-sector investment.

For almost three decades, the region experienced stunning economic growth accompanied by massive investments in health and education that were widely credited with contributing to smaller family size, higher living standards and improvements in women's status.

The crisis in Indonesia, Malaysia, the Philippines and Thailand has increased poverty and unemployment, lowered educational participation, and reduced funding for social programmes, including population and reproductive health programmes. Preliminary evidence suggests that the region's remarkable development gains of the past three decades are being reversed as a result — and that women and children are suffering the most.

The crisis has significantly increased school dropout rates throughout the region. Unemployment has risen sharply, particularly in Indonesia, and disproportionately in the sectors in which women work. Urban job losses have reversed traditional rural-urban migration patterns and created a new class of urban poor.

Falling real incomes and rising prices of food and other basic commodities have combined to produce increased incidence of malnutrition in babies and young children in parts of Indonesia.

The crisis has exacerbated the harsh realities of women's lives and made gender equality and equity a more distant goal. Rising poverty has increased pressure on women to enter the commercial sex industry; and because of a lack of accessible services, these new recruits are poorly equipped to protect themselves from sexually transmitted diseases including HIV/AIDS.

Reproductive health programmes continue to suffer as budgetary priority is given to addressing hunger, rising poverty, unemployment and social disruption. Preliminary evidence suggests unsafe abortions have increased, while opportunities for post-abortion counselling in family planning are limited. There have been cutbacks in health promotion and medical service activities, including HIV/AIDS and STD prevention and treatment programmes. The problem of inadequate access to reproductive health services for adolescents, especially girls, has intensified.

Source: UNFPA. 1999. *South-east Asian Populations in Crisis: Challenges to the Implementation of the ICPD Programme of Action.* New York: UNFPA.

---

increased in the less-developed regions as a whole, but has lagged in the least-developed countries.

Periodic inquiries by the United Nations Population Division have shown a growing number of developing countries initiating actions in the areas of fertility and mortality reduction, and increasing policy interest in migration and population age structure.

The ICPD Programme of Action reconfirmed the vital role of population in social development strategies, and stressed the dynamic relationships among population, social and economic development, poverty alleviation, the quality of the environment, and the empowerment of women.

Increased recognition of the role of population within development has led nearly half of all developing countries to review their policies since 1994.[1] More than a third have updated their population policies to be consistent with ICPD objectives or have integrated factors such as the quality of health care, gender equality and the improvement of demographic information systems into long-term development plans.

Sixty-seven countries have made policy changes affirming a commitment to reproductive health and rights.

In Africa, many countries have focused their reviews on broad population and development issues, including poverty alleviation and human resource development. In Asia and the Pacific, more countries have focused on reproductive health and mortality.[2] Fewer countries in Latin America have engaged in policy reviews but those that have, including Mexico, Jamaica, the Dominican Republic, Panama, and Trinidad and Tobago, have addressed local concerns like population distribution and the needs of underserved young and old populations.

Two thirds of all countries have introduced policy or legislative measures to promote gender equality and equity and women's empowerment. Nearly all countries in Latin America have introduced policy measures, legislation or institutional changes to protect women's rights; nearly half have national policy or action plans. More than half the Asian countries and a number of African countries (including Botswana, Burundi, Namibia, Nigeria, South Africa, Uganda and Zambia) have acted to protect women's rights in areas such as inheritance, property and employment.

Many countries have strengthened laws and policies to combat gender-based violence including rape, incest, domestic violence and female genital mutilation. Fifteen African States have banned FGM, including Senegal, Burkina Faso, Côte d'Ivoire, Ghana and Togo.

Nearly two thirds of Latin America and the Caribbean countries but fewer than half of all countries have acted to increase men's responsibility for their sexual and reproductive behaviour and their social and family roles, through measures such as employment legislation and child-support laws.

Sixty-seven countries have made policy changes affirming a commitment to reproductive rights and reproductive health. Over 40 have incorporated this perspective in the provision of health services. Many countries have acted to improve the quality of reproductive health services (see Chapter 3). Nearly half the countries in the world have taken new measures to address adolescent reproductive health needs, often in collaboration with NGOs and the private sector.

Policy evaluations are now undertaken with a wider variety of inputs than previously. During the 1970s and 1980s many countries developed wide-ranging population and development policies but specified action plans primarily in maternal and child health and family planning. Population sections of national development plans have implications for policies in many areas including employment, education, health, food security, environmental protection, women's social participation, community action and local administration. Legal and policy changes in these diverse areas will be more successful if those with a stake in the policy reviews have accurate, timely information on population trends and their implications.

At the same time, the ongoing policy re-evaluations are taking place in a dramatically changing social and political environment. Most developing countries have undertaken economic reforms aimed at liberalizing domestic and global economic relations. The key reforms have been the disinvestment of the State from the production sector, the adoption of non-expansionist monetary and fiscal policies, the reduction of state administration, trade liberalization and the deregulation of the labour market. In this new environment, countries and firms have to become more efficient and competitive. There is a danger that smaller and poorer economies will become even more marginalized.

Domestic economic reforms and globalization have affected population migration and population redistribution, particularly through accelerating urbanization trends. These population changes in turn impact on poverty, health, housing and environmental factors, with implications for population policies and development strategies.

Such changes have affected the role of national planning institutions. Increased reliance on the private sector for development activities and decentralization of authority and administration make it imperative that there be wider access to policy-relevant demographic information and analyses. Public institutions have an important role to play in providing the information needed to develop and sustain competitive economic systems.

Policy priorities have been an important focus of the five-year review of implementation of the ICPD Programme of Action. Expert round tables, technical meetings and regional population and development conferences have addressed population and economic development, international migration, civil society, reproductive health and rights, and population ageing.

Population Continues to Grow, and to Grow Older

At the beginning of the 20th century, the world's population was approximately 1.5 billion; by 1960 it had doubled; and by late 1999, it had quadrupled to 6 billion. The global population is unlikely ever again to grow as fast as it has in the last few decades and particularly the past 12 years, in which a billion people were added.

Annual additions to the global population rose from 47 million per year in 1950–1955 to a peak of 86 million in 1985–1990. This unprecedented growth was the net result of faster declines in mortality than in fertility, both from initially high levels. As a consequence, the fourth, fifth and sixth billion marks in global population were achieved in only 14, 13 and 12 years, respectively.[3]

Today, a "demographic transition" from high fertility and mortality to low fertility and mortality is under way or has already occurred in much of the world. In many respects, the less-developed regions are now about halfway through this transition, approximately where the more-developed regions were a half-century ago.

Death Rate Cut by Half

The most important story behind the rapid rise from 3 to 6 billion people since 1960 is the unprecedented drop in mortality. This trend actually began in the 19th and early 20th century, but intensified after World War II as basic sanitation, clean drinking water and modern health care became more available in larger areas of the world. Since 1950, the death rate has been cut in half, from about 20 to fewer than 10 deaths per year per thousand people. At the same time, average global life expectancy has risen from 46 to 66 years.

Death rates have fallen by half since 1950, accounting for much of the rapid growth of world population.

The world's population is healthier from infancy through old age than it ever has been. Global infant mortality has fallen by two thirds since 1950, from 155 per thousand live births to 57 per thousand; this rate is projected to be reduced by a further two thirds by 2050. Maternal mortality has also declined, but much more slowly and less generally (see Chapter 3). Other promising health trends include improvements in immunization levels and health education.

One positive effect of lengthening life-spans and better medical treatment has been that the annual number of deaths actually fell by more than 10 per cent between 1955 and 1975 even as nearly 1.5 billion people were added to the world population. Subsequently the number of deaths began to increase. The current number of deaths per year, 52 million, is the same as in 1950, when the population was less than half the size it is today.

Death rates have declined substantially in the less-developed regions since 1950, but have remained roughly constant in the more-developed regions because of their greater proportion of older people.

Fertility is Declining, but Unevenly

The number of births per year rose from 98 million in 1950 to a peak of 134 million in the late 1980s, and is projected to remain just under 130 million for the next 20 years while death rates slowly rise as the global population ages.

Although only a very few countries have declining populations, 61 countries (with about 44 per cent of the world's population) already have below-replacement fertility rates (less than 2.1 births per woman). The number of such countries is projected to grow to 87 by 2015, encompassing about two thirds of the world's population.

On the other hand, in 2050, 130 countries will still have positive growth rates, 44 of them above 1 per cent per year, about the rate observed in more-developed regions in 1965.

In 1950-1955, the average fertility rate in the more-developed regions was 2.8 children per woman; it has since dropped to 1.6 and is projected to begin a slow rise, to 1.8, by the middle of next century. In the less-developed regions, the fertility rate was almost 6.2 in 1950; it was slightly less than 3 by 1999, and is projected to fall to less than 2.1 by 2045.

Fertility has declined most quickly in Latin America and Asia, less rapidly in

Lower Population Projections: Good News and Bad

The United Nations Population Division's latest projection for global population in 2050, 8.9 billion (medium variant), is substantially lower than its 1996 projection of 9.4 billion. In response, some commentators have raised concerns about "missing" people. This is misleading.

The major reason for the lower projection is good news: global fertility rates have declined more rapidly than expected, as health care, including reproductive health, has improved faster than anticipated, and men and women have chosen to have smaller families.

About one third of the reduction in long-range population projections, however, is due to increasing mortality rates in sub-Saharan Africa and parts of the Indian subcontinent. The most important factor is HIV/AIDS, which is spreading much faster than previously anticipated.

In addition, United Nations demographers have adopted more refined projection techniques. Formerly, it was assumed that countries with below-replacement fertility rates would return to replacement levels by 2050. The current assumption is that these countries will have fertility rates of 1.7 to 1.9 births per woman (rather than 2.1) by 2050.

North Africa and the Middle East, and much more slowly in sub-Saharan Africa. Asia's fertility fell sharply in the last 50 years, from 5.9 to 2.6 children per woman. Sub-Saharan Africa's has dropped much more slowly, from 6.5 to 5.5. Latin America and the Caribbean have seen a decline from 5.9 to 2.7, North Africa and Western Asia from 6.6 to 3.5.

Europe's fertility rate fell from 2.6 to 1.4, well below replacement level. On the other hand, Northern America's fertility fell from 3.5 in 1950-1955 to 1.8 in the late 1970s, and then rebounded to the 1.9 to 2.0 range, where it has remained. It is projected to stay around 1.9 to the middle of the 21st century.

Variations between and within regions, and among different population groups within countries, remain considerable. Some nations, such as Brazil and the Republic of Korea, have moved swiftly to near-replacement level or below; others, such as Nigeria and Guatemala, have seen only a slight fall in fertility rates. However, the pace of decline has varied dramatically in different parts of both Brazil and Nigeria.

Hopes of finding a simple and consistent explanation for the demographic transition[4] have been repeatedly dashed by the realities of data on local experiences.[5] In fact, there is no tight statistical link between development indicators and fertility rates, and the reasons for fertility decline are widely debated by demographers, economists and policy makers. While development is still considered an important factor, it remains unclear why fertility transitions occur earlier in some places than others. The pace of development does not appear to affect the initiation or the rate of fertility transition. However, once a transition has begun, fertility declines more rapidly in countries with higher levels of development.[6]

Helping women and men to realize their family size desires

It seems clear that the family size desires of men and women are influenced by a variety of factors: mortality declines; increased social opportunity, especially for women; employment opportunities; incomes; and educational access. Women and men cannot realize these desires, however, without the means to translate social opportunity and choice into action. The creation and progressive strengthening of population programmes over the last 30 years[7] — along with the development and distribution of more-effective and safer forms of contraception — has been a crucial catalyst in reducing fertility rates.[8] Population programmes have been given credit for about half the decline in fertility since 1960.[9] Since the ICPD, they have adopted an approach based on individual rights and needs.

The spread of information about family planning techniques and new ideas about social issues — including the rights of women to reproductive health and equality of opportunity — facilitates the fertility transition.[10] Discussion and debate among relatives, friends and neighbours, the diffusion of ideas between communities, and mass media images trigger changes in preferences and fertility behaviour. This may explain why fertility changes often occur more rapidly in countries where various channels connect communities and individuals, and more slowly where such social interaction is more difficult. If this is the case, improving communications could help to speed up the fertility transition where it has been slow.[11]

Population programmes have been crucial in reducing fertility rates in the past 30 years.

Predicting what will happen at the end of the fertility transition in a particular country — whether fertility will stabilize at below, near or above replacement level, or will bounce back upwards or have some other unstable pattern — remains a critical challenge for demographers.

Changing assumptions about future fertility

In late 1998, the United Nations Population Division released its latest population projections for the world, regions and countries through 2050 (see page 3). The Population Division produces new projections every two years based on updated population data and revisions in projection methodology. In the case of the 1998 Revision, both factors had a substantial impact on the long-range projections.[12]

It is now projected that the global population will rise to between 7.3 and 10.7 billion by 2050; the medium variant projection, considered most likely, is 8.9 billion. The key assumptions that create these results are global fertility rates, which are projected to fall to between 2.5 and 1.6 births per woman by 2050. Under the medium variant scenario, it is assumed that the fertility rate for every country in the less-developed regions will drop to exactly 2.1 by 2050. For the more-developed regions, national fertility rates are projected to reach between 1.7 and 1.9, depending on the country.

These assumptions point out the inherent uncertainties of population projections. The United Nations projections have a record of successive adjustment to new information and considerable long-term accuracy. However, it does not seem very likely that the Congo, Nicaragua and Kazakhstan, with current fertility rates of 6.1, 4.4, and 2.3 births per woman, respectively, will all have identical fertility rates of 2.1 in 2050. Similarly, it is by no means certain that Italy's fertility rate will rise from 1.2 to 1.7, or the United States' rate will drop from 2.0 to 1.9 by 2050, as the medium variant projection assumes. National fertility rates will remain unpredictable over the long run. Demographers, at institutions including the United Nations, are undertaking analyses to improve or place scientific certainty bounds around projection scenarios.[13]

Education Levels and Fertility Declines

Throughout the developing world, literacy and years of schooling have increased for both males and females over the last four decades.[14] Demographers and sociologists have observed that improved education for women and girls is closely related to improvements in health and to falling fertility rates.

Educated women are more likely to use contraception and tend to marry later.

Enrolment ratios have increased since 1960 in all regions and at all education levels, especially at the primary level.[15] In sub-Saharan Africa, however, primary school enrolment was still only 75 per cent in 1995 and has actually decreased since 1980. Enrolment has also declined recently in other countries affected by financial crises.[16]

In low- and middle-income countries, 53 per cent of the relevant age group were enrolled in secondary schools in 1995, up from 41 per cent in 1980. This compares poorly with the high-income countries, where virtually all children have some secondary education, and 35 per cent have some tertiary education (college and graduate school).

The limited data available on years of schooling illustrate the stark contrasts that persist. For instance, in Burundi, men and women have had, on average, 5 and 4 years of schooling, respectively. In Costa Rica, those numbers are 10 and 9 years, respectively; in Canada, 18 and 17 years.

There is still a significant gender gap among both teachers and pupils in low-income countries, but the situation is improving: 42 per cent of students in 1980 were female, 44 per cent in 1995; 32 per cent of teachers in 1980 were female, 39 per cent in 1995. In middle- and high-income countries, the gender balance for pupils and teachers is much closer — men still outnumber women in both groups, but only by a few percentage points.

To foster the social development of girls, some countries have begun to promote girls' education through waiving fees, or providing a small payment or food allocation for girls' attendance, and by adapting the school system to facilitate their participation. Since 1990, the Bangladesh Rural Advancement Committee has, for example, created over 30,000 schools that offer non-formal primary education; 70 per cent of the pupils are girls.[17]

FIGURE 2: Educational Attainment by Gender, Region

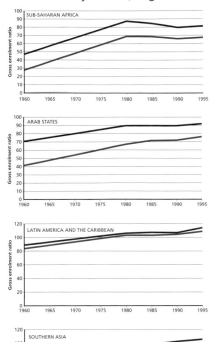

Gross enrolment ratio
SUB-SAHARAN AFRICA
1960 1965 1970 1975 1980 1985 1990 1995

Gross enrolment ratio
ARAB STATES
1960 1965 1970 1975 1980 1985 1990 1995

Gross enrolment ratio
LATIN AMERICA AND THE CARIBBEAN
1960 1965 1970 1975 1980 1985 1990 1995

Gross enrolment ratio
SOUTHERN ASIA
1960 1965 1970 1975 1980 1985 1990 1995

■ Female ■ Male

Note: Gross primary enrolment ratios indicate the number of students per 100 individuals in the appropriate age group. Ratios over 100 are due to late starts, interrupted schooling or grade repetition.

Source: UNESCO. *World Education Report 1995.*

Recent analyses undertaken for the World Bank[18] reveal significant income-based differentials in child enrolment, and distinct regional patterns of enrolment in poor populations. For example, in Latin America, there is near universal enrolment of the poor in first grade but then substantial dropout grade by grade, while in South Asia and Western and Central Africa the poor mostly do not enrol.

Differences between the rich and the poor in median years of schooling completed vary considerably across countries, ranging from only one year to as many as 10. The effect of adult income levels exceeds male-female differentials in many settings.[19] Poor girls, however, suffer from a double disadvantage that can severely restrict their opportunities.

Nearly one out of four adults in the world, around 1 billion people, cannot read, write or do simple arithmetic.[20]

Education leads to smaller, healthier families

One of the strongest and most consistent relationships in demography is between mothers' education and infant mortality — the children of women with more years of schooling are much more likely to survive infancy.[21] More-educated mothers have better health care, marry later and are significantly more likely to use contraception to space their children. They have better skills for obtaining and evaluating information on health care, disease prevention and nutrition. They also have better access to resources, through earning opportunities and marriage, and can manage them better. They are more likely to recognize the advantages of educating their children.

The relationship between women's education and fertility is also complex, but the underlying pattern in most countries is that the more years of schooling a woman has, the fewer children she is likely to have. In a small number of countries, particularly in sub-Saharan Africa, fertility rises slightly with the first few years of women's schooling, then falls with subsequent years of education.[22] In all recent studies,

FIGURE 3: Regional Trends in Age Structure

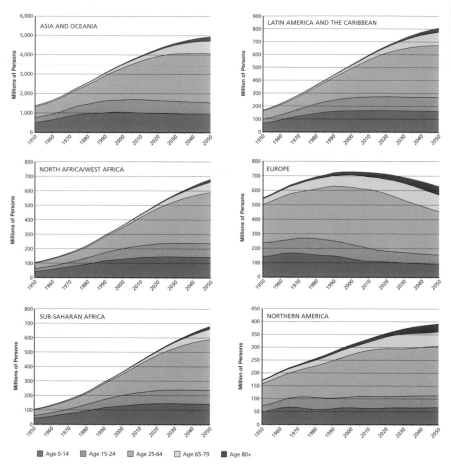

Age 0-14 ■ Age 15-24 ■ Age 25-64 □ Age 65-79 ■ Age 80+

Source: United Nations. *Sex and Age Quinquennial 1950-2050 (The 1998 Revision).*

additional secondary education for women correlates with lower fertility.

Educated women are more likely to use modern methods of contraception, and they tend to marry later. Educated parents of both sexes also generally desire smaller families than those with less education, and educated women tend to act on that reproductive preference for fewer children. In other words,

women with more schooling are more likely to have the number of children they say they want.[23]

According to a study of Egyptian families, the educational aspirations that women and men have for their children, particularly their daughters, are significant factors in how many children they desire. Parents who hope for better education for their female children tend to want smaller families, perhaps so that they can provide more fully for the offspring they have.[24]

Women of all levels of education and economic status take steps to choose the number and spacing of their children. Their ability to do so is a function of not only education, but also circumstance, resources and custom.[25] Population programmes help provide the means.

Ageing Populations

A gradual ageing of the global population in the decades to come is all but certain. The reasons for this trend reflect the substantial human progress of this century — lowered infant and child mortality; better nutrition, education, health care and access to family planning; and longer life expectancies.[26]

This transition is already well under way in the more-developed regions, where the median age has risen from 29 in 1950 to 38 today and is projected to plateau at around 46 by 2050. In the less-developed regions, this process is just beginning; since 1950, the median age has fluctuated between 19 and 24 (its current level). Africa, the world's most rapidly growing region, is also the youngest, with a median age of only 18. The median age in all the less-developed regions is projected to begin a gradual rise to 37 by 2050.

There is every reason to believe that societies in both the more- and less-developed regions can adjust to the higher median age of their inhabitants and the increasing ratio of old to young people. Yet undoubtedly this new era will present distinct challenges. The world's people have never been this healthy or

lived this long. In 1950, average life expectancy globally was 46 years; in 2050 average life expectancy is projected to be 76, and the median age is projected to be 38.

Countries in more-developed regions are already coming to grips with this unprecedented transition and the issues that it presents with respect to the labour pool, care for the elderly, and the potential for population decline.

Around the world, but particularly in the more-developed regions, countries with ageing populations will face challenges providing support and medical care for the elderly. The percentage of young dependants will decline, but the proportion of older dependants will increase.

The Youth Factor

Today, as a result of high fertility in the recent past, there are more young people than ever — over 1 billion between ages 15 and 24. They are entering their peak childbearing years. In all developing countries, the proportion of the population aged 15-24 peaked around 1985 at 21 per cent. Between 1995 and 2050, it will decline from 19 to 14 per cent, but actual numbers will grow from 859 million to 1.06 billion

These numbers ensure continued population growth, even if young people choose to have smaller families than their parents had. Indeed, populations would continue to grow for several decades even if "replacement-level" fertility were reached immediately.

This phenomenon, known as "population momentum", will account for up to two thirds of the projected population growth worldwide, more in countries

BOX 9

Devastating Impact of HIV/AIDS in Africa

New estimates of the prevalence of HIV/AIDS indicate that the epidemic is more serious than was previously thought. Estimates released in 1998 by UNAIDS and the World Health Organization indicate that global HIV infections increased 10 per cent in 1998 to 33.4 million people worldwide. Last year alone, an estimated 5.8 million people contracted the virus that causes AIDS.

Using UNAIDS estimates of the number of people currently infected, the United Nations Population Division last year produced projections of future HIV prevalence rates and the likely demographic impact in 34 of the most-affected countries (29 of them in Africa), accounting for 85 per cent of currently infected persons and 91 per cent of all AIDS deaths to date.

In the 29 African countries, the average life expectancy at birth is currently seven years less than it would have been in the absence of AIDS. The average life expectancy in the nine countries with an adult HIV prevalence of 10 per cent or more (Botswana, Kenya, Malawi, Mozambique, Namibia, Rwanda, South Africa, Zambia and Zimbabwe) is estimated to be 48 years, 10 years less than it would have been in the absence of AIDS. However, the population is not expected to decline in any of these countries.

In Botswana, with the world's highest HIV/AIDS prevalence rates — one of every four adults is infected — life expectancy has fallen from 61 years in the late 1980s to 47 today, and is expected to plunge to 38 by 2005-2010. Botswana's population by 2015 may be 23 per cent smaller than it would have been in the absence of AIDS. Nevertheless, because of continuing high fertility, the population is still expected to nearly double between 1995 and 2050.

In Zimbabwe, the second-hardest-hit country, one in five adults is infected. Estimated life expectancy at birth is 44 years and will fall to 41 in 2000-2005, 25 years less than what would be expected in the absence of AIDS. Population growth has fallen to 1.4 per cent; it would be 2.4 per cent without AIDS. Zimbabwe's population in 2015 is expected to be 19 per cent lower than it would have been in the absence of the epidemic.

FIGURE 4: The Impact of AIDS in Sub-Saharan Africa: Population Projections with and without AIDS in the 29 Most-affected Countries, 1980-2050

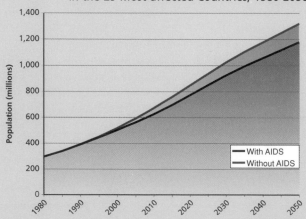

Source: United Nations. *World Population Prospects: The 1998 Revision.*

where fertility has fallen most quickly. In Thailand, for instance, where three people out of ten are under age 15, the population is projected to grow by 19 per cent between 1999 and 2025, even though the average couple is having fewer than two children. Raising the average age at which women have their first child from 18 to 23 would reduce population momentum by over 40 per cent.

Globally, lower birth rates create the strong possibility of a "demographic bonus" in the less-developed regions in the next couple of decades, as a "bulge" of young people grow up and become part of the work force while fewer children are born. If enough employment opportunities can be created, these new workers could well result in greater productivity and economic development, and generate substantial revenues for health care, education and social security.[27] There is every reason to believe that societies in both the more- and less-developed regions will benefit from this change.

The Impact of AIDS

HIV/AIDS is now the leading cause of death in Africa and the fourth most common cause of death worldwide.[28] The Joint United Nations Programme on HIV/AIDS (UNAIDS) estimates that 33.4 million people were HIV-positive as of December 1998 and 2.5 million died of the disease in 1998 — 2 million in Africa. One half of all new HIV infections are in young people between ages 15 and 24.

It is estimated that 95 per cent of those infected live in developing countries, and two thirds live in sub-Saharan Africa, where 8.0 per cent of adults aged 15-49 are HIV-positive. AIDS has a terrible effect on individuals and communities, as it strikes down working people, orphans children, and places huge strains on health care and social systems.

In demographic terms, the future effect of AIDS is likely to be relatively limited on the global scale, but it will have a devastating impact on several African countries. Because of high fertility rates, most sub-Saharan African countries are still expected to experience population growth, but for the most-afflicted nations the pace will be much slower than it would be without the epidemic.[29]

In many countries, AIDS has erased decades of progress in reducing child mortality and increasing life expectancy. In addition to increasing mortality, HIV/AIDS can also affect demographic change by reducing the fertility of women who are infected and influencing age at marriage, sexual behaviour and contraceptive use.

The course of this epidemic, both globally and in particular countries, is still to be determined. There are some hopeful signs — infection and mortality rates are falling in a number of countries, though they are continuing to rise in others. The development of the epidemic in South and East Asia, and particularly in India and China, is a particular cause of concern.[30] Slowing and stopping the spread of AIDS will require improvements in comprehensive reproductive health care, as well as better public education about the risks and consequences of HIV infection.

Prospects for Low-fertility Countries

An active debate is under way within the demographic community about the prospects for future fertility in current (and projected) low-fertility countries. There may well be a "bottom" for fertility rates for each society, a point after which rates will begin to rise again, but demographers clearly cannot make that kind of prediction with any certainty.

One school of thought holds that below-replacement fertility is unlikely to persist very long. In this view, projected fertility declines may be overstated because methods of measuring current fertility rates do not capture completed fertility trends when more younger women are delaying childbearing until later in their lives.[31]

For instance, in the United States and Sweden, the fertility rate dropped well below replacement in the 1970s and 1980s but rose again to above 2.0 in the early 1990s. On the other hand, the fertility rate in Italy also dropped below replacement in the late 1970s and has continued to fall, reaching 1.2 by the late 1990s.

It is considered significant that completed fertility among those who have any children remains above the replacement level in most European countries. Statements of desired fertility also remain at or above replacement level. Measured fertility declines might stop when the age of marriage ceases to increase unless desired fertility falls.

Another school of thought holds that below-replacement fertility, particularly in Europe, has become well-established and associated with continuing declines in desired family size.[32]

It is not clear, meanwhile, that all countries will reach below-replacement fertility. In some countries, fertility declines

have stalled at levels above replacement level.[33]

Changing Distribution of World Population

Population growth will be concentrated in certain regions; elsewhere, human numbers will stablize or even decline. Within countries, populations will continue to shift from rural to urban areas, while becoming increasingly older and better educated. Migration between countries will be an increasingly important factor in international relations and the composition of national populations.

The world's urban population is growing by 60 million a year.

Regional Distribution Changing

As the global population has doubled over the past 40 years, the shifts in geographical distribution of that population have been equally remarkable. In 1960, 2.1 billion of the world's 3 billion people lived in less-developed regions (70 per cent of the global population). By late 1999, the less-developed regions had grown to 4.8 billion (80 per cent); 98 per cent of the projected growth of the world population by 2025 will occur in these regions.

Africa, with an average fertility rate exceeding five children per woman during the entire period, has grown the fastest among regions. There are almost three times as many Africans alive today (767 million) as there were in 1960. Asia, by far the most populous region, has more than doubled in size (to over 3.6 billion), as has Latin America and the

Caribbean. In contrast, the population of Northern America has grown by only 50 per cent, and Europe's has increased by only 20 per cent and is now roughly stable.

Africa's share of global population is projected to rise to 20 per cent in 2050 (from only 9 per cent in 1960), while Europe's share is projected to decline from 20 to 7 per cent over that same period. In 1960 Africa had less than half the population of Europe; in 2050 it may be approaching three times as many people.

The altered balance of population distribution among regions does not in itself pose a problem, so long as development progresses everywhere and population growth is balanced by the development of social and economic capacity. The challenge remains to create conditions that will enable countries in all regions to adopt policies and strategies that foster equitable development.

Global Trend Towards Urbanization

The movement of people towards cities has accelerated in the past 40 years, particularly in the less-developed regions, and the share of the global population living in urban areas has increased from one third in 1960 to 47 per cent (2.8 billion people) in 1999. The world's urban population is now growing by 60 million persons per year, about three times the increase in the rural population.[34]

Increasing urbanization results about equally from births in urban areas and from the continued movement of people from the rural surround. These forces are also feeding the sprawl of urban areas as formerly rural peri-urban settlements become incorporated into nearby cities and as secondary cities, linked by commerce to larger urban centres, grow larger.[35]

The proportion of people in developing countries who live in cities has almost doubled since 1960 (from less than 22 per cent to more than 40 per cent), while in more-developed regions the urban share has grown from 61 per cent to 76 per cent. There is a significant association between this population movement from rural to urban areas and declines in average family size.

Asia and Africa remain the least urbanized of the developing regions (less than 38 per cent each). Latin America and the Caribbean is more than 75 per cent urban, a level almost equal to those in Europe, Northern America and Japan (all are between 75 and 79 per cent).

Urbanization is projected to continue well into the next century. By 2030, it is expected that nearly 5 billion (61 per cent) of the world's 8.1 billion people will live in cities. The less-developed regions will be more than 57 per cent urban. Latin America and the Caribbean will actually have a greater percentage of inhabitants living in cities than Europe will.

Cities and towns have become the engines of social change in all regions. Their rapid growth presents opportunities for future development but also serious challenges. Urban population growth has outpaced the development of employment, housing,

In 1960, two cities had populations over 10 million. Today there are 17 such cities. By 2015 there will be 26.

FIGURE 5: Regional Distribution of Population, 1950-2050

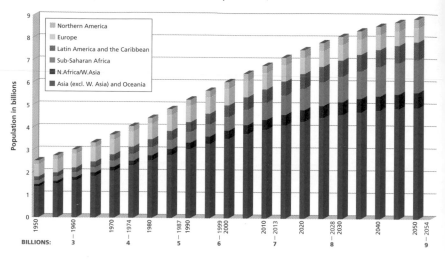

Legend:
- Northern America
- Europe
- Latin America and the Caribbean
- Sub-Saharan Africa
- N.Africa/W.Asia
- Asia (excl. W. Asia) and Oceania

Y-axis: Population in billions

X-axis: 1950, 1960, 1970, 1974, 1980, 1987, 1990, 1999, 2000, 2010, 2013, 2020, 2028, 2030, 2040, 2050, 2054

BILLIONS: 3, 4, 5, 6, 7, 8, 9

Source: United Nations. *World Population Prospects. The 1998 Revision.*

services and the rest of the social and physical infrastructure. Poverty persists in urban and peri-urban areas, suggesting a failure of policies to ensure an equitable distribution of the fruits of development. Numbers of poor women, in particular, have increased, both in urban areas (where work opportunities remain limited) and in rural areas (where women are increasingly being left behind by husbands or children seeking urban opportunities).

As people have moved towards and into cities, information has flowed outward. Better communication and transportation now link urban and rural areas both economically and socially. The result is that the ecological and sociological "footprint" of cities has spread over ever-wider areas, creating an urban-rural continuum of communities that share some aspects of each lifestyle. Fewer and fewer places on the planet are unaffected by the dynamics of cities.

The spread of mass media has also blurred the rural-urban divide. New ideas, points of reference, and life possibilities are becoming more widely recognized, appreciated and sought. This phenomenon has affected health care, including reproductive health, in many ways. For instance, radio and television programmes that discuss gender equity, family size preference and family planning options are now reaching formerly isolated rural populations. This can create demand for services, higher contraceptive use, and fewer unwanted pregnancies.[36]

Globally, the number of cities with 10 million or more inhabitants is increasing rapidly, and most of these new "megacities" are in the less-developed regions. In 1960, only New York and Tokyo had more than 10 million people. By 1999, the number of megacities had grown to 17, 13 in less-developed regions. It is projected that there will be

26 megacities by 2015, 22 in less-developed regions (18 will be in Asia); more than 10 per cent of the world's population will live in these cities, up from just 1.7 per cent in megacities in 1950.

International Migration

International migration is becoming a more visible and important issue in international relations and in national self-concepts.

Globally, the number of international migrants increased from 75 million to 120 million between 1965 and 1990, keeping pace with population growth. As a result, the proportion of migrants worldwide has remained around 2 per cent of the total population.[37] In 1990, international migrants were 4.5 per cent of the population in developed countries and 1.6 per cent in developing countries.

These global estimates mask important difficulties in measuring migration. Only a handful of countries regularly count inflows of foreigners and returning citizens, so it is virtually impossible to make estimates of foreign-born migrants except via periodic censuses. Migrants sometimes avoid or are neglected by census-takers, and they are counted or classified in different ways by different countries. Migration is often the result of conflict, persecution or weather-related hardship, and as a result it fluctuates greatly from year to year and may be accompanied by chaos, making precise counts difficult.

Virtually all countries have been the destination of some migration in this century of rapid and universal transportation. Recipient countries for migrants have become more diverse since 1965, both in terms of the number of migrants they receive and their share of total population.[38] The number of coun-

FIGURE 6: World Urbanization Trends, 1950-2030

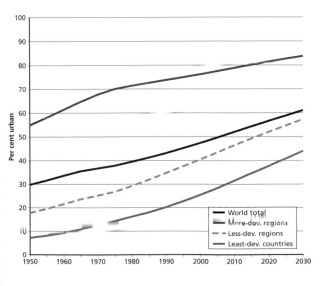

Per cent urban

- ■— World total
- ■— More-dev. regions
- - - Less-dev. regions
- ■— Least-dev. countries

Source: United Nations. *World Urbanization Prospects (The 1996 Revision).*

tries with a migrant population of 300,000 or greater increased by more than 50 per cent between 1965 and 1990.

The percentage of women migrants has increased in recent decades, to 48 per cent of all international migrants in 1990.[39] Most women who migrate for employment tend to be concentrated in low-status jobs, and many are particularly vulnerable to exploitation and harassment.

The globalization of capital and trade flows is causing unpredictable changes in the fortunes of developing countries, as investment capital rapidly moves in and out of fragile economies. In turn, these movements drive both internal and international migration. The growing informalization of the economies of many countries has also intensified the interaction between irregular employment and irregular migration.

Increased immigration has been recommended by a number of demographers and economists as a means of balancing the effects of fertility decline and the resultant ageing of the population. For instance, a labour shortage in Japan has been met by expanding the number of foreigners (including descendants of former Japanese emigrants) who can be admitted to the country. Between 1985 and 1995, the legally resident foreign population in Japan increased by 60 per cent, and the number of undocumented aliens also grew.[40]

The economic effects of migration run both ways. Throughout the world, remittances by migrants from more- to less-developed countries remain an important mechanism through which international migration influences development.

Population Growth and Environmental Concerns

Environmental limits to growth?

The 200-year-old apocalyptic prediction[41] and more recent warnings[42] that human population growth would eventually outstrip the capacity of land to produce food have thankfully not come true. Human ingenuity and continued improvements in agricultural technology have thus far ensured that global food supplies have grown at least as fast as population. But as the 20th century ends scientists are still pondering the underlying question: are there environmental limits to the number of people and the quality of life that the earth can support?

Because natural conditions, technology, and consumption and distribution patterns are constantly in flux, and there is no universal agreement as to the definition of "carrying capacity", it is unlikely that there will ever be a definitive answer. Most scientists who have pondered the issue have predicted that there are natural limits, but the predicted limits fall within a broad range: 4-16 billion people.[43] What will happen as human population approaches those limits, either globally or locally, will depend on human choices — about lifestyles, environmental protection and equity.

Water, Land and Food

In sub-Saharan Africa and parts of the Indian subcontinent, which together contain about one third of the world's population, mortality rates are increasing and are responsible for one third of the fall in long-range population projections.[44] Birth rates in these areas have not declined as rapidly as they have elsewhere, and aquifer depletion and decreasing per capita crop land are central players in projected demographic and resource trends.

An urgent concern for many rapidly growing countries is shrinking crop land per person. In Nigeria, per capita grain land is projected to shrink from 0.15 to 0.07 hectares per person by 2050. Pakistan's grain land per person would drop from 0.09 to 0.04 hectares in the same period.[45] Countries that currently have 0.03 hectares or less of grain land per capita, such as South Korea and Japan, import about 70 per cent of their grain. Because global per capita grain output has been stagnant for more than a decade and world grain carryover stocks have been dropping, these trends pose critical questions as to their effects on international food supply, markets and distribution. Will

---

BOX 10

One Person in Four May Face Water Shortages by 2050

One fourth of the world's people are likely to live in countries facing chronic or recurring shortages of fresh water by the year 2050, according to a recent study by Population Action International.

Already, more than 430 million people — 8 per cent of the world's population — are living in countries affected by water stress or outright scarcity, the study found. That is expected to increase four-fold, to nearly 2 billion by mid-century.

There is already fierce national competition over water for irrigation and power generation — most notably in the Tigris-Euphrates and Nile river basins. Along the Euphrates River, Iraq, Syria and Turkey compete for one primary water source. This competition will worsen if, as projected, their combined populations grow by some 50 per cent over the next 30 years.

While the Middle East and North Africa are the regions most affected by water scarcity today, sub-Saharan Africa will be increasingly affected over the next half century, as its population doubles or even triples. In several countries, water supply is already inadequate to meet the demands of a growing industrial sector. Within the next 10 years, Kenya, Morocco, Rwanda, Somalia and South Africa are projected to join the ranks of the water scarce.

On the other hand, slower population growth than previously projected may reduce the threat of water shortages and allow more time to develop conservation strategies in India, Pakistan, Jordan, Sri Lanka and El Salvador, the study found.

The study is based on a widely used methodology developed by Swedish hydrologist Malin Falkenmark. It holds that countries with annual, renewable fresh water of less than 1,700 cubic metres per person will begin to experience periodic or regular "water stress" and those with less than 1,000 cubic metres per person will face "water scarcity", hindering economic development and threatening human health and well-being.

Source: Population Action International. 1997. *Sustaining Water, Easing Scarcity: A Second Update.* Washington, D.C.

the countries and people who need to import food in the future be able to afford it?

In many parts of both the more- and less-developed world, water demand already substantially exceeds the sustainable supply.[46] In India, for instance, water withdrawals are now estimated to be twice the rate of aquifer recharge, with the result that water tables are falling by one to three metres per year.[47] The International Water Management Institute estimates that the eventual lack of water for irrigation could cut India's grain production by 25 per cent. This is a grave issue in a country whose population reached 1 billion in 1999 and is expanding at the rate of 18 million per year, and where 53 per cent of all children are currently malnourished.[48]

Rising population has reduced world grain area per person by 50 per cent since 1950.[49] Little viable agricultural land remains unexploited, and existing crop land continues to be lost to industrial expansion and residential development. If the quantity of agricultural land is not increasing, grain yield improvements must keep pace with population growth, currently 1.3 per cent per year, just to maintain the status quo in per capita food output.

Continued improvements in agricultural technology and crop productivity may well result in further increases in grain yield, but these are not likely to be on the same scale as the gains made in the "green revolution" of recent decades; there is evidence that there may be biological limits to crop yields.

Climate Change, Natural Resource Degradation and Biodiversity

Continued population growth will affect other environmental trends, including collapsing fisheries, shrinking forests, rising temperatures, and the wholesale loss of plant and animal species.

Global warming is a wild card inextricably linked to population-related issues, including fuel consumption, land use trade-offs and the potential limits on food and water supplies. The Intergovernmental Panel on Climate Change, a United Nations-sponsored panel of 2,500 scientists, has projected that, if current greenhouse gas emission trends continue, the mean global surface temperature will rise from 1 to 3.5 degrees Celsius in the next century.[50] The panel's "best estimate" scenario projects a sea-level rise of 15 to 95 centimetres by 2100. The ecological and human impacts of rising oceans would include increased flooding, coastal erosion, and salinization of aquifers and coastal crop land, and the displacement of millions of people living near the coast.

Patterns of precipitation are also likely to change, which combined with increased average temperatures, could substantially alter the relative agricultural productivity of different regions.

Greenhouse gas emissions are closely linked to both population increases and development. Slower population growth would make emission reductions easier to achieve and provide more options for adaptation to climate change.

CHAPTER 3

Reproductive Health and Reproductive Rights

The Reproductive Health Approach

The ICPD accepted that the right to reproductive and sexual health is included among human rights. Human rights related to reproductive health include:

Reproductive decision-making on the basis of equality between women and men, including voluntary choice in marriage and determination of the number, timing and spacing of one's children;

∎

Sexual and reproductive security, including freedom from sexual violence and coercion, and the right to privacy.

Nigel Dickenson / Still Pictures

Photo: Mother and children in Brazilian slum. Millions of poor women worldwide want to delay or avoid pregnancy but lack access to family planning information and services.

Universal access to quality services is a primary means to reproductive health and a central goal of the ICPD Programme of Action.

The need is as pressing today as it was in 1994:

Maternal mortality. More than 585,000 women die each year as a result of pregnancy.[1] At least 7 million women suffer serious health problems and as many as 50 million suffer some health consequences after childbirth.

> *More than 585,000 women die each year as a result of pregnancy.*

Unsafe abortion. Some 20 million unsafe abortions take place in developing countries each year and as many as 70,000 women die, accounting for 13 per cent of maternal deaths.[2]

Sexually transmitted disease. There are over 330 million cases of treatable sexually transmitted diseases each year; 33.4 million persons are living with HIV/AIDS, and there are 5.8 million new infections each year, or 11 a minute.

Unwanted pregnancy. Of the nearly 175 million pregnancies each year, as many as half are unwanted or ill-timed. Around 120 million women do not want another birth within the next two years or at all and are not using any method of family planning because of lack of access, information or the support of families and communities. Over 350 million women do not have a choice of safe and effective contraceptive methods. Of the nearly 130 million births each year, more than 60 million are not assisted by a trained delivery attendant: over 98 per cent of these are in less-developed regions.

Gender-based violence exacts a heavy toll on mental and physical health. Millions of women require medical attention or otherwise suffer the impact of rape, incest and domestic violence; fear of violence inhibits discussion and constrains the health choices and life opportunities of many millions more. More than half of all women will suffer some form of gender-based violence at some time in their lives. More than 2 million girls and women per year become involved in the sex industry, often from coercion or desperation. Two million girls and young women are at risk of female genital mutilation (FGM) each year and an estimated 130 million are already affected.

Adolescent reproductive health. Young girls are at particular risk of reproductive ill-health. More than 14 million adolescent girls give birth each year. A large proportion of these pregnancies are unwanted, and it is estimated by the World Health Organization (WHO) that as many as 4.4 million abortions are sought by adolescent girls each year. Harmful practices such as FGM and child marriage followed by expectations of early childbearing further increase the risk of reproductive ill-health.

In most countries, family planning is still the central component of reproductive health services. Five years after the ICPD, however, all countries have taken some steps to ensure access to comprehensive sexual and reproductive health information and services. Many countries have adopted the ICPD definition of reproductive health and are moving towards a client-centred approach to meeting reproductive health needs. In some countries, implementation is moving ahead rapidly.[3]

Less progress has been made in implementing integrated reproductive health programmes, because service delivery infrastructures are weak and human and financial resources are lacking.[4]

Components of Reproductive Health

Key elements of reproductive health include:

- Meeting the need for family planning;

- Ensuring maternal health and reducing infant mortality;

- Preventing and treating STDs, including HIV/AIDS;

- Eliminating traditional practices such as FGM that are harmful to women's reproductive health and well-being.

Countries are increasingly including other elements such as prevention of cervical and breast cancer and infertility.

Family Planning

Although contraceptive use in developing countries increased by 1.2 percentage points per annum between 1990 and 1995,[5] the needs of about 20-25 per cent of couples are still not being met. The level of unmet need was highest in sub-Saharan Africa (29 per cent) and lowest in Latin America and the Caribbean (18 and 20 per cent). Access to family planning has increased dramatically in some countries, including Nepal and Bhutan. In the Central Asian countries of Kazakhstan, Uzbekistan and Kyrgyzstan,

59 per cent of married couples practise family planning today, compared to less than 20 per cent in 1990.

Many countries have sought to expand the range of contraceptive methods; to improve information and counselling services to enable contraceptive choice with an understanding of the individual's sexuality, partner and social relations, and gender issues; and to provide more complete and accurate information and counselling on side-effects and their management.

Studies in eight countries found that while women and men are convinced that using family planning and having smaller families provides economic and health benefits, there are many ways programmes can improve.[6] The studies found, for example, that side-effects of certain contraceptive methods are more of a problem for women than providers realize.

In all countries, the quality of services can be improved. More specifically, contraceptive counsellors must take into consideration that gender norms may be a barrier for both women and men seeking family planning. Particularly where family planning services are new, where women tend to use contraception clandestinely, and where discontinuation because of side-effects is a problem, networks of established users are needed to help new users. Men and other influential family members should be educated to help them support women's contraceptive choices.

The diversification of service providers has increased access to family planning services in many parts of the world. For example, over 16 million couples in 55 countries benefited from social marketing in 1997, compared to 14.4 million in 1996, an increase of 13 per cent. Social marketing programmes sold 937 million condoms in 1997, an increase of 20 per cent over sales in 1996. The big increases were the result of the social marketing programmes in India and Indonesia. Increasing sales of condoms also indicate their importance for the prevention of STDs, including HIV/AIDS.

Two new methods of contraception, once-a-month injectables and the female condom, have become available since 1994. Shelf life for the female condom has been extended from three to five years, making it more available to women worldwide. Emergency contraception, a high dose of an oral contraceptive used by women after intercourse to prevent unwanted pregnancy, has also become more accessible since 1994.

Methods for male fertility regulation remain severely inadequate, however. More investment is needed in research and development of new methods for men as well as female-controlled barrier methods to prevent both STD transmission and pregnancy. Donor support for contraceptives has increased 15 per cent between 1994 and 1996.[7]

The best way to reduce abortion is to prevent unwanted pregnancy by making family planning more accessible.

Safe Motherhood

The ICPD and other United Nations conferences have stressed that maternal mortality is both a development issue and a human rights issue. The ICPD target is to halve 1990 levels of maternal mortality by the year 2000 — this will not be reached — and reduce them by a further one half by 2015 (specifically, in countries with the highest levels of mortality, to below 60 per 100,000 live births).

In 1997, a meeting organized by the Inter-Agency Group on Safe Motherhood[8] concluded that training traditional birth attendants, providing antenatal screening for high-risk pregnant women, and providing simple birth kits are not enough. Needed are skilled midwives, especially in rural areas, with regulations that permit them to carry out necessary procedures and post-partum care; adequate supplies and equipment backed up by transport in case of emergency; and supportive supervision and monitoring.[9]

Although progress has been disappointing, some governments have invested in safe motherhood. Tunisia, for example, began its Safe Motherhood Programme in 1990. After the ICPD, the Ministry of Health developed a comprehensive reproductive health strategy including other components such as testing for reproductive cancers, and prevention and management of STDs. In Indonesia, the coverage of antenatal care

and supervised delivery significantly improved after the Government developed a programme to train more than 54,000 community midwives.

In Ghana, Uganda, Nigeria and Vietnam midwives have been trained in life-saving skills, using a training package developed by the American College of Nurse-Midwives that includes risk assessment, problem solving and clinical management needed to save the lives of women during obstetric emergencies. Uganda's Ministry of Health launched a pilot project in one district to establish a sustainable referral system that included strengthening referral facilities, communication and transportation. As a result, obstetric referrals and caesarean sections increased threefold between 1995 and 1996.

Improving maternal health calls for better health facilities, logistic systems

---

Japan Approves Use of Oral Contraceptives

Nine years after a group of pharmaceutical companies applied to Japan's Ministry of Health and Welfare to market a low-dosage contraceptive pill, the ministry's Central Pharmaceutical Affairs Council gave its approval in June 1999. Japan had been the only member of the United Nations to ban oral contraceptives.

The lifting of the ban is expected to play a large role in preventing unwanted pregnancies. The most popular form of family planning in Japan today is condoms, and women have had limited recourse to methods that they could fully control. A shift to more effective methods could also reduce the reported 340,000 abortions each year.

Concern about a possible reduction in condom use and increased exposure to sexually transmitted diseases including HIV/AIDS was one reason for the pharmaceutical council's reluctance to approve the pill. The Health and Welfare Ministry hopes to keep STD cases to a minimum by obligating women to obtain a doctor's prescription and by creating a manual for physicians and users.

The pill's approval could accelerate a trend towards fuller equality between the sexes. A strengthened Equal Employment Opportunity Act came into force in April, and a gender equality law is expected to be passed later in 1999.

Source: "Pill Approved", *Mainichi Shimbun*, 4 June 1999.

and training to ensure appropriate and effective care. Another challenge is to overcome social barriers to access, including improving men's understanding of their roles and responsibilities in women's health. This could be critical: a recent survey in Nepal, for example, found that the decision to seek care for pregnant or post-partum women was most often made by husbands, followed by mothers-in-law; the women themselves were seldom involved in the decision.[10]

Preventing and managing unsafe abortion

Most countries are strengthening efforts to prevent unwanted pregnancies and some are working systematically to reduce the health impact of unsafe abortion, which remains a major public health concern.

Permitting legal access to abortion is a matter for national decision: according to the United Nations Population Division, 189 of the world's 193 countries allow abortion to save the life of the woman, 120 allow it to preserve the woman's physical health, 122 to preserve mental health, 83 in cases of rape or incest, 76 in instances of foetal impairment, 63 for economic or social reasons, and 52 upon request.[11] Since 1985, at least 19 countries have enacted new abortion laws or modified existing laws to expand women's access and choice.[12]

Studies and programme experience show that the best way to reduce abortion is to prevent unwanted pregnancy by making family planning services more accessible. For example, in the three Central Asian republics of Kazakhstan, Uzbekistan and Kyrgyzstan, better availability of services and information has increased the use of modern contracep-

BOX 13

ICPD Programme of Action on Unsafe Abortion

Paragraph 8.25 of the ICPD Programme of Action states:

"In no case should abortion be promoted as a method of family planning. All Governments and relevant intergovernmental and non-governmental organizations are urged to strengthen their commitment to women's health, to deal with the health impact of unsafe abortion as a major public health concern and to reduce the recourse to abortion through expanded and improved family-planning services. Prevention of unwanted pregnancies must always be given the highest priority and every attempt should be made to eliminate the need for abortion. Women who have unwanted pregnancies should have ready access to reliable information and compassionate counselling. Any measures or changes related to abortion within the health system can only be determined at the national or local level according to the national legislative process. In circumstances where abortion is not against the law, such abortion should be safe. In all cases, women should have access to quality services for the management of complications arising from abortion. Post-abortion counselling, education and family-planning services should be offered promptly, which will also help to avoid repeat abortions."

The United Nations General Assembly's 1999 fifth-year review of the ICPD also agreed that "in circumstances where abortion is not against the law, health systems should train and equip health-service providers and should take measures to ensure that such abortion is safe and accessible."

Source: United Nations 1999. *Report of the Ad Hoc Committee of the Whole of the Twenty-first Special Session of the General Assembly* (A/S-21/5/Add.1).

tion by 30-50 per cent since 1990, and abortion rates have declined by as much as half.[13]

A number of countries (including Kenya, Tanzania, Uganda, Ethiopia, Ghana, Zambia, Nigeria, Malawi, South Africa, Zimbabwe, Mexico, Brazil, Ecuador, Peru, Paraguay, Chile, Nicaragua, Honduras, Guatemala, El Salvador) focus on reducing the health impact of unsafe abortion through post-abortion care. Some countries are training midwives and other providers to offer post-abortion care, including links to family planning services in order to prevent repeat abortions.

In Ghana, a study showed that midwives at primary- and secondary-level health facilities could successfully offer post-abortion care. The study demonstrated improved referral to area hospitals, better community education about unsafe abortion and improved standing of these midwives within their communities.[14]

HIV/AIDS and Sexually Transmitted Diseases

HIV/AIDS is an even more serious public health problem than ICPD foresaw, particularly in sub-Saharan Africa, with 20.8 million, or close to 70 per cent of HIV-infected people (see box in Chapter 2 on the demographic impact of HIV/AIDS).

In spite of these figures, several countries still do not recognize HIV as a major threat to public health. In addition, there are approximately 333 million new cases of sexually transmitted diseases each year, but many countries do not have the capacity to diagnose and treat them. Having an untreated sexually transmitted disease can increase the risk of HIV infection tenfold.

In 1996, the Joint United Nations Programme on HIV/AIDS (UNAIDS) became operational, with a mission to lead, strengthen and support an expanded response to prevent the transmission of HIV, provide care and support, and reduce the vulnerability of individuals and communities to HIV/AIDS. UNAIDS works in full partnership with its United Nations co-sponsors, including UNFPA. Since January 1996, UNAIDS theme groups have been established in most countries to increase the effectiveness of United Nations efforts and to coordinate with national AIDS programmes. NGOs are also members of the theme groups or technical working groups in Brazil, Cambodia, Chile, Democratic Republic of the Congo, Indonesia, Jordan, Rwanda, Swaziland and Viet Nam, among others.

Reproductive health programmes can reduce levels of STDs including HIV/AIDS, by: providing information and counselling in critical issues such as sexuality, gender roles and power imbalances between women and men, and mother-to-child transmission of HIV; distributing female and male condoms; diagnosing and treating STDs; developing strategies for contact tracing; and referring people infected with HIV for further services.

Though health care staff do not generally receive sufficient training and support to provide STD/HIV/AIDS information and services, case studies in four countries in Africa (Burkina Faso, Côte d'Ivoire, Uganda and Zambia) found that providers were willing to discuss sexuality and STDs with clients, and could understand the need to identify

3

BOX 14

Combating STDs and HIV in Uganda

In Africa, HIV/AIDS is not only a personal and family tragedy but also a major challenge to social and economic development. In Uganda the epidemic has prompted an unprecedented national response. It is estimated that 1.5 million Ugandans out of a total population of 21 million are infected and that 1 million children have been orphaned by AIDS deaths. Families, the labour force, and leadership in society depend on the age group most affected (ages 15 to 50).

The government recognized early the devastating impact that AIDS would have on development, and the key role of sexually transmitted diseases in its spread. The national programme began in the late 1980s with financial support from major donors including UNFPA. It involves several government ministries and includes public information campaigns, research, voluntary testing and counselling, safe blood for transfusions, school health programmes, home-based care of people living with AIDS, and a nationwide campaign to treat STDs.

The STD/HIV control programme emphasizes outreach to underserved groups, especially young people, and involvement of parents and local communities. The Uganda AIDS Commission, which coordinates policies and programmes throughout the country, includes parliamentarians, government officials and religious leaders.

These efforts are producing results. Almost the entire adult population is now aware of the dangers of HIV and, in some parts of the country, rates of infection among women seeking prenatal care have decreased by one third or more. The campaign has led to greater openness in dealing with sexual health problems and has increased the commitment of the government to providing reproductive health services to every segment of the population. HIV prevalence rates among young people are now stabilizing.

Source: L. Ashford and C. Makinson. 1999. *Reproductive Health in Policy and Practice.* Washington, DC: Population Reference Bureau.

individuals at risk of sexually transmitted infections.[15]

According to a 1997 UNAIDS review of the impact of preventive education on the sexual behaviour of young people, good-quality sex education helps adolescents delay sexual intercourse and increase safe sexual practices.[16] Since the ICPD, in 64 countries, support has been provided for the integration of HIV/AIDS prevention modules into in-school and out-of-school education programmes.

In Swaziland, SHAPE (Swaziland Schools HIV/AIDS and Population Education Programme) was launched in 1990 to prevent the spread of HIV/AIDS and to reduce teenage pregnancy in school pupils aged 14 to 19. In 1997, as

a result of the ICPD, the programme was also introduced in primary schools. The programme has improved knowledge and attitudes more than behaviour.[17]

Currently, an estimated 27 million people do not know they are HIV positive, underlining the need for simple methods to diagnose HIV. Countries have already introduced the female condom, the only female-controlled barrier method that can protect against HIV transmission, as a result of the organized demand of women's groups and in recognition of the importance of supporting women's control in this area.

A study in Thailand found that a one-month course of an antiretroviral drug effectively halved the risk of HIV infection in non-breast-fed infants born to HIV-positive women. UNAIDS, UNFPA, UNICEF and WHO in 1998 began offering voluntary and confidential HIV counselling and testing to pregnant women in 11 pilot countries. Those who learn they are infected are provided with anti-retroviral drugs, better birth care, safe infant feeding methods and post-natal counselling, and family planning.[18]

Female Genital Mutilation

The ICPD called for an end to female genital mutilation, the partial or total removal of external female genitalia, a practice that has severe health and psychological consequences. Worldwide, an estimated 130 million girls and women have undergone some form of FGM, and each year 2 million are believed to be at risk. Most are in 28 countries in Africa and the Arabian Peninsula. Thousands die each year as a result of FGM, from infections and haemorrhaging or in childbirth.

The Programme of Action called on governments "to prohibit female genital mutilation wherever it exists and to give vigorous support to efforts among non-governmental and community organizations and religious institutions to eliminate such practices".[19]

In the past several years, efforts to combat FGM have gained strength, largely as the result of advocacy efforts by NGOs such as the national chapters of the Inter-African Committee on Traditional Practices. In early 1999, Senegal joined Burkina Faso, Central African Republic, Côte d'Ivoire, Djibouti, Ghana, Guinea, Tanzania and Togo in outlawing the practice. Similar laws have been proposed in Benin, Nigeria and Uganda.[20] In Egypt, the Supreme Court in 1997 upheld a ministerial decree prohibiting physician-assisted FGM as well as a 1959 law criminalizing all FGM in the country.

The practice of FGM is deeply rooted within cultural traditions and eliminating it will require persistent efforts. Some older women insist on having their daughters or granddaughters mutilated to maintain their eligibility for marriage. That is a perception they share with some younger women who fear social rejection if they do not undergo the procedure.

Various culturally sensitive initiatives have been undertaken to show that harmful traditional practices can change without compromising values. In Uganda, the Reproductive, Educative and Community Health (REACH) programme has substituted gift-giving and public celebration of womanhood for FGM rituals. The campaign, begun in 1995, reduced FGM in the country's Kapchorwa district by 36 per cent in 1996. The UNFPA-supported programme involves the community at all levels, especially the local elders. Those who practise FGM are given training as traditional birth attendants.

Similarly, the Kenyan women's organization Maendeleo ya Wanawake encourages alternatives to the coming-of-age rituals surrounding FGM, emphasizing positive cultural traditions of the community. Those who perform FGM are helped to find alternate means of support.

In Senegal and Egypt, campaigns of women's rights activists have successfully advocated changing laws and practices regarding FGM. Egypt's FGM Task Force, composed of activists, researchers, doctors and feminists, played

BOX 15

Literacy Group Spurs Fight against FGM in Senegal

Since 1997, dozens of Senegalese communities have declared an end to female genital mutilation and begun pressing others to join them. Their actions helped spur the country's president and parliament to outlaw the practice in January 1999. The grass-roots activism grew out of the efforts of an NGO called Tostan ("Breakthrough"). The group was started 11 years ago, as a literacy and skills training programme for women, built around group discussions. With funding from UNICEF, it hired villagers to teach the classes and published workbooks in local languages.

Rather than confront issues like FGM directly, Tostan took several months before broaching the subject of women's health. Even then, according to Molly Melching, the group's founder and director, "We never spoke about sexuality. We only spoke about health, and rights." Villagers say months of discussing infections, childbirth and sexual pain inevitably led them to question FGM. "Tostan taught us that it is OK to speak our mind," said one woman.

Men as well as women have been involved. "It is a hard thing to admit that something you and your ancestors had considered right all your life is in fact wrong," said one of the elders who participated in discussions.

Melching believes that making a political issue of FGM, or declaring it a barbaric act, does not convince many people. "These women really love their children," she said. Although Tostan stresses human rights violations, the health risks are what everyone understands. Criminalizing those who still practise FGM, Melching fears, "could drive the practice underground".

By getting entire villages to sign on to the plan to stop performing FGM, Tostan's approach ensures that no one carries a stigma. The movement has gained momentum as news of the villagers' decision spreads across the country.

One woman who lost her job as a circumciser was persuaded to abandon the practice after months of discussion. "When I learned that this might cause sterility and infections, I didn't want to be the cause of all that," she said.

Source: Vivienne Walt. 11 June 1998. "Circumcising a Ritual". Los Angeles Times-Washington Post News Service.

a pivotal role in broadening debate on the sensitive and charged issue of FGM and creating a climate for a political ban on the practice. Government-NGO coalitions are emerging in Mali and Nigeria to fight FGM and violence against women.[21]

Providing Reproductive Health Services

Policy Change since the ICPD

Policy change is essential to the ICPD goal of universal access to reproductive health care, and more than 40 countries have taken action in this area since the ICPD. Some have developed comprehensive national reproductive health policies, while others have dealt only with specific aspects. Response to a wide range of interests and a multisectoral approach have been the cornerstones of successful policy-making.

India has replaced a decades-old policy of target-based family planning with a client-centred approach to individuals' reproductive health needs, providing a range of services including an expanded choice of contraceptive methods. This policy change started before the ICPD and was the result of a sustained effort by women's health advocates and others calling for change.

In Bangladesh, a government/donor/ NGO consortium developed the 1997 Health and Population Sector Strategy, which affirms the principles of the ICPD. Zambia also involved local health districts, NGOs, donor agencies and private institutions in formulating its new national reproductive health policy. Zambia's extensive needs assessment process addressed gender issues, including male involvement, as well as the allocation of resources for its implementation. In South Africa, NGOs provided key support to provincial governments in the development of a women's health policy.

Brazil developed a comprehensive women's health policy a decade before the ICPD, but progress to integrate reproductive health into the Unified Health System accelerated after Cairo. In 1997, the Congress passed a National Family Planning Law that approved all temporary contraceptive methods and recognized voluntary sterilization as a standard procedure.

In China, a UNFPA-supported programme is being introduced in 32 counties spread throughout the country, using a client-centred approach as recommended by the ICPD. If it is successful, it will be expanded to more parts of the country.[22]

In addition to broad national policies, countries such as Ghana and Nepal have developed operational policies to guide implementation of reproductive health at the service delivery level. Many countries are lifting regulations and policies that limit access to family planning services, for example, spousal authorization, marital status and age limits. By

1997, however, 14 countries still required spousal authorization for women to receive contraceptive services, and 60 more required spousal authorization for permanent methods.[23]

Less progress has been made in reorienting polices to address gender issues. Some policies recognize the need to enhance women's status, but few specifically address gender and the power relations that affect reproductive decisions.

Health Sector Reform and Decentralization

Reproductive health is often being addressed at the same time as reforms in the whole health sector, and while many countries are decentralizing authority for health services from central ministries to local governments. As part of health-sector reform, most countries are defining priority areas for investment, and making hard choices about allocation of scarce human, financial and institutional resources.

Health-sector reform and decentralization do not guarantee that reproductive health will be included — sometimes the opposite occurs.[24] But the process is expected generally to be more cost-effective and result in greater consumer satisfaction, which in turn is likely to lead to more effective use of information and services.

Countries such as India, Bangladesh, Mexico, the Philippines, South Africa and Zambia that have adopted an essential services package approach as part of their health sector reform have generally included reproductive health. For example, Bangladesh's essential services package includes: maternal health (antenatal,

BOX 16

Health-sector Reform

Health services in many countries have deteriorated because of poor management, organization and infrastructure maintenance, while concentration on big hospitals in city centres has starved district and primary levels of resources. Reforms include decentralized management, innovations in financing and cost containment, and reorganization of service delivery. There is a new emphasis on primary and preventive health care, including reproductive health.

Health managers are being asked to implement the reproductive health approach and overall health reform at the same time. The two are potentially complementary and mutually reinforcing; in fact, the effectiveness of the reproductive health services is an excellent measure of how well the entire health system is working. Nevertheless, there are possible areas of conflict in design and implementation arising from the way in which services were delivered prior to reform and the way in which the transition is managed.

Financing and managing reproductive health care is one of the main challenges of reform. Managers from a specific programme area such as family planning, immunization or STD control see reproductive health as a call to integrate their service with other components of the package. On the other hand, when health reformers react to the call for a reproductive health approach, they may view integrated reproductive health services as yet another "vertical" program.

Source: T. Merrick, 1999. "Delivering Reproductive Health Services in Health Reform Settings: Challenges and Opportunities." Work in progress.

delivery and postnatal care, menstrual regulation and post-abortion complication care); adolescent health; family planning; management and prevention/control of reproductive tract infections, STDs and HIV/AIDS; and child health.

Decentralization has often meant giving more responsibility to local authorities without providing adequate resources.[25] Some local governments have started charging even for basic services, which has meant that the poor, especially women and children, often go without health care. It is important that health-sector reform and decentralization should not neglect the ICPD commitment to better reproductive health care.

Integrating and Broadening Reproductive Health Programmes

Most countries are at a critical point as they seek to establish integrated, comprehensive reproductive health programmes. It would be counterproductive to raise the expectations of potential clients without providing the services to meet them, but there are problems regarding both the process and resources to implement it, and there are few models to follow.

Many countries are testing ways of integrating reproductive health services, including Bangladesh, Brazil, Cambodia, Egypt, Ghana, India, Jamaica, Mexico, Peru, the Philippines, Senegal, South Africa, Thailand, Tunisia, Uganda, Viet Nam and Zambia. The integration of family planning and maternal and child health under a common institutional umbrella has been the most common change: Egypt, for example, has centralized reproductive health services under a newly established Ministry of Health and Population. Some countries have linked the components of reproductive health through referrals, particularly among family planning, maternal and child health and STD/HIV/AIDS services.

Many countries are testing ways of integrating reproductive health services.

Many countries in sub-Saharan Africa have begun to integrate STD/HIV/AIDS services into their clinic-based maternal and child health and family planning services, as the lowest-cost way to reach the highest possible proportion of sexually active women and their partners. However, analysis of Botswana, Ghana, Kenya, Zambia and Zimbabwe shortly after service integration found that virtually no family planning clients underwent any diagnosis or treatment for STD/HIV/AIDS. On the positive side the analysis showed that it would be feasible at least to provide information about symptoms, modes of transmission and protective behaviour.[26]

Integrating institutional and administrative structures is a particular challenge. In many countries, particularly in Asia, family planning and health have been managed separately for years, at considerable cost, but changes since the ICPD have been nominal, because of bureaucratic inertia and differences in programming, training and evaluation regimes. Countries have made more progress in integration at the service delivery level. Many already had integrated family planning and maternal and child health services and since the ICPD have integrated them further, both with each other and with STD and HIV/AIDS prevention, screening and treatment. For example, services might be offered at the same place by different providers, or by the same personnel but on different days.

3

BOX 17

Integration at the Service Delivery Level in Uganda

In Uganda, health centres now provide family planning, prenatal and post-natal care, STD/HIV counselling, nutrition education, and childhood immunization services every day, rather than different services on designated days. The nurses see integration as a mixed blessing: their workload has increased without a comparable increase in pay, but integration saves time for them and their clients, and the increased responsibilities have enhanced their status.

Integration has proceeded more rapidly in health centres than in hospitals, though the latter provide a wider range of services. Reports show that more clients are using the family planning and STD treatment services (both previously stigmatized in some communities), now that they are part of a broader package. Integration of reproductive health services in primary health centres has made life easier for some women. One pregnant woman said, "These days it is much better coming here because they treat for everything daily…. It saves money."

Source: L. Ashford and C. Makinson. 1999. *Reproductive Health in Policy and Practice*. Washington, D.C.: Population Reference Bureau.

Some countries such as Bangladesh provide their essential services package at one location. Others, as in India, refer clients to delivery points where they can find higher levels of service, for example, STD treatment or emergency obstetric care.

Additional training can broaden the scope of services at existing service delivery points without formal integration: countries such as Mozambique and Burkina Faso have added the prevention and management of STDs including HIV/AIDS to family planning services. Many other African countries are linking family planning and STD/HIV/AIDS programmes by a system of mutual referrals.

NGO Provision of Reproductive Health Services

In some countries, NGOs, most notably the International Planned Parenthood-affiliated family planning associations and women's organizations, have more flexibility than government services in redesigning programmes and training staff. NGOs can work more easily than government organizations in especially sensitive areas such as adolescent issues and gender-based violence. In countries such as Bangladesh, Colombia, Mexico, Peru and Jamaica, NGOs have taken the lead in expanding reproductive health services and particularly in providing family planning in the context of reproductive health, and in providing services to men and adolescents.

In Zambia, NGOs fully support the health reform process, and the government recognizes NGOs as important partners within the health sector. NGOs are in a position to push the reproductive health agenda forward, to be more inno-

vative and creative, to take risks, and to test models for integrated service delivery that the public sector can duplicate on a larger scale. Donors and technical assistance organizations that feel restricted by public-sector requirements can promote their ideas to NGOs.[27]

Sri Lanka has a tradition of community-based organizations involved in development and NGOs are linked through an NGO secretariat. The four major NGOs in family planning, including the Family Planning Association of Sri Lanka, are seen as pioneers and continue to work in family planning, reproductive health education, advocacy and service delivery. UNFPA is funding them to serve as umbrella organizations for smaller community-based organizations that provide education and information on family planning. UNFPA is also funding four other NGOs to include linking reproductive health to other development issues and reaching new target groups with information.[28]

NGO services can be less cost-effective than those of government programmes. The cost per person served is sometimes higher because of overhead, capacity-development costs, diseconomies of scale and small catchment areas. Still, since the ICPD, NGOs have played an increasingly important role in implementing the Programme of Action.

In a recent eight-country study on implementing the ICPD Programme of Action, NGOs were consistently cited as being more successful than governments in providing reproductive health services. Respondents in Bangladesh, India, Nepal, Jordan, Ghana, Senegal, Jamaica and Peru noted that the streamlined bureaucracies of NGOs give them the flexibility to expand services.[29]

NGOs have taken the lead to train providers to offer client-centred services. For example, Jamaica's family planning association, FAMPLAN, recently participated in a project to integrate family planning and STD services. The project, which included training to help providers break down their biases against STD clients, succeeded in increasing condom use without lengthening the time providers spent with clients.

NGOs have also been credited as being close to communities. In Peru, community-level NGOs working with women have a better conception than government institutions of women's broad reproductive health needs. These NGOs work closely with health personnel to ensure that women are referred to appropriate organizations for help.

NGOs do not provide services on the same scale as public-sector agencies in most countries; in fact, their size is probably a virtue in allowing NGOs the flexibility to change services. In Senegal, large NGOs provide a small proportion of family planning and reproductive health services, but respondents said that they set standards for quality, and contribute technical expertise to the programme. Smaller NGOs are also a significant factor in communities, particularly in working on AIDS and FGM. Community women's organizations carry out education in reproductive health, a task for which public-sector health workers often lack time.

For now, however, NGOs do not have the resources needed to offer all components of reproductive health. Increasing resources channelled to NGOs would be a good investment in most countries. However, if NGOs were expected to grow to serve the same number of clients and the same geographic locations as public-sector agencies, they might lose their ability to provide flexible and innovative programming.

Increasing Access to Quality Services

The quality of reproductive health care is critical in determining whether the service meets clients' expectations, and thus whether they use it. The components of quality of care are well established. Clients need a choice of contraceptive methods, accurate and complete information, technically competent care, good interaction with providers, continuity of care, and a constellation of related services.[30] These elements apply equally to other components of reproductive health care.

Clients want respect, accurate information, and services that are convenient, prompt and reliable.

If they are given a choice, clients will use facilities and providers that offer the best care as they perceive it. Studies around the world[31] suggest that clients want:

- **Respect**, friendliness, courtesy, confidentiality and privacy.

- **Understanding** on the part of providers of each clients' situation and needs.

- **Complete and accurate information**. Clients want all the facts, particularly about side-effects of contraceptives.

- **Technical competence.** Clients judge the cleanliness of clinics, the thoroughness of examinations and the types of medication they are given, and ultimately whether their needs are met or their problems resolved.

- **Access and continuity of care and supplies.** Clients want convenient, prompt and reliable services and supplies. Access also means that services are reliable, affordable and without barriers.

- **Fairness.** Clients want providers to offer information and services to everyone regardless of class or ethnicity.

- **Results.** Clients are frustrated when they are told to wait or come back on a different day, or when their complaints are dismissed as unimportant.

Studies in Jamaica, Kenya and Malawi have shown that clients generally have a less positive view than providers about issues such as waiting time, time spent in consultation and the information given to clients.[32] Research in Morocco revealed communication problems because of hierarchical modes of communication and a lack of female providers. Women said they wanted more information on contraceptive methods and to be offered more than just family planning.[33] In Albania, some service delivery sites miss the opportunity to provide women with family planning. In one study, a woman said, "The staff in our area don't serve women; they say, 'We are only here for children's vaccinations.' So we don't know where to get this service [family planning]."[34]

Quality matters to clients. In Bolivia, women in one study said they would travel further to clinics that provide better quality. One woman said, "I prefer to go there [to the family planning clinic] even though it is far away. They talk to me; they explain things. Even though I have to pay, it's okay."[35] In Tanzania, another study found the same thing: quality of care affected clients' choice of service site.[36] In Bangladesh, one woman noted, "I sat down in a chair inside [the provider's] office, and she asked me . . . my name [and] many things about myself — how many children I had, how old my youngest child was, and so on…. She told me that if I had any serious problems in the meantime, I should come and see her again . . . . [She] behaved nicely with me. There were no difficulties."[37]

Research and evaluation can indicate what is needed to make improvements. The Population Council's Situation Analysis studies in sub-Saharan Africa have shown how underutilization of resources diminishes quality and choice of clients.[38] Elsewhere quality suffers from shortages of water, electricity, equipment or supplies, particularly in rural areas. In Pakistan, for example, only around 10 per cent of the population have access to family planning services.[39] In Burkina Faso and Côte d'Ivoire, family planning is not available in many health facilities.

The Situation Analysis studies in five sub-Saharan African countries revealed several missed opportunities for quality care[40]:

- New clients seeking to space pregnancies were not offered all the spacing methods available at the clinic, restricting clients' ability to choose the most appropriate or desirable method;

- Providers generally do not make use of information materials which could improve clients' understanding and assist them in making more fully informed decisions;

- Most providers see three or fewer family planning clients per day, suggesting that they could increase the length of client visits, improve the quality of information given, and expand the reproductive health service offered;

- Providers commonly make use of equipment such as blood pressure machines and ultrasound when available; however, they often do not wash their hands during pelvic exams, even when clean water and gloves are in the exam room, putting clients at risk of infection;

- Providers frequently do not inquire about the number and frequency of partners or whether the partner is included in the decision to seek contraception, and are thus unable to assess or recommend appropriate methods;

- The ability of a given method to protect against sexually transmitted infections, and in particular the dual-protection benefit of condoms, is rarely discussed.

Improving quality of care requires a focus on the process of service delivery, including communication and information sharing; establishing minimal standards for procedures and examinations; and ensuring that clients receive the service appropriate to their needs. Some countries, such as Sri Lanka, have made considerable progress, beginning before the ICPD, to provide high-quality, client-centred-integrated services.

Studies show that improvements in quality can be made at a reasonable cost; without them, people will not come to or continue using the service.[41] Using various tools,[42] family planning providers and supervisors worldwide are being trained to improve quality of care, thereby creating commitment to solve problems as they arise.

Among the team-based approaches to making improvements, one of the most widely used tools is COPE (Client-Oriented and Provider Efficient), developed by the NGO AVSC International. COPE uses a set of simple self-assessment tools developed for workers in family planning clinics and for their supervisors. Staff members analyse client flow through the clinic, conduct interviews with clients, and complete a questionnaire on every aspect of service delivery. COPE has been used in over 35 countries. An evaluation of COPE at 11 clinics in Africa found that teams had solved 64 of 109 problems identified through the COPE process.[43]

Training in quality of care creates commitment to solve problems as they arise. Principles include treating the client well, providing the client's preferred method, individualizing care, aiming for dynamic interaction, avoiding information overload and using and providing memory aids.[44] Some countries, such as India, Nepal, Egypt, Indonesia and Jordan, are instituting quality assurance procedures related to reproductive health services. Egypt's Gold Star programme is one of the largest quality assurance programmes in the world. It is designed not only to improve the quality of services, but also to create the expectation of better services. About half of all Ministry of Health and Population units reached Gold Star status by the end of 1998.[45]

In many countries, a lack of trained staff has slowed the expansion of reproductive health services.

In many countries, public-sector providers also work part-time as private providers. Many clients prefer private-sector providers because their clinics are more convenient and less crowded, and because they believe that private-sector providers are more competent; but this perception may be more myth than reality. Mechanisms to improve quality in the private sector have included continuing medical education on reproductive health topics, setting up quality assurance mechanisms, and strengthening linkages between public- and private-sector providers.

Communication and Education

Well-designed communication strengthens good programmes, but information without services only produces dissatisfaction. Raising awareness about reproductive health is not the same as increasing the use of the services. In many countries, information campaigns are developed without the involvement of local providers, communities and representatives from the target groups. Messages are usually designed for adult women and ignore key target groups like men, adolescents, newlyweds and opinion leaders.

Communication strategies are not always well linked with services: a campaign may raise awareness of contraception but may not say where to find it; or motivate potential clients before the services are available. Information, education and communication (IEC) strategies about reproductive health must go well beyond sensitization to provide information about how to avoid reproductive tract infections, unwanted pregnancies and obstetrical complications, for example. Hot lines and radio call-in shows are good for providing accurate and confidential information. Combining several media also reinforces messages.[46]

Information and education strategies about reproductive health and population and development issues must advance beyond awareness raising. Policy makers and programme beneficiaries alike need information that will help them to make decisions and act on them. They need information about, for example, the risks of STDs, the danger signs of a difficult pregnancy, and available methods of contraception. They also need information on who can provide assistance, where services are to be found and what kinds of treatment they can expect and have a right to demand.

This information must reach everyone who needs it. The mass media are useful for giving practical information,[47] but traditional and local communication channels are also needed. So are non-governmental organizations and community groups.

Countries wishing to improve IEC do not have to start from scratch: in many countries there is a wealth of

Communication linked to services is an essential part of reproductive health programmes. Left, Mexican health assistant gives talk to village women about family planning and reproductive health.

material, especially for family planning, maternal and child health, STDs/AIDS and sexuality, that could be adapted to reproductive health. For example, the Philippines strategy and guidebook for family planning IEC is excellent and could be easily modified to fit reproductive health.

Developing Human Resources

In many countries, particularly in sub-Saharan Africa, but also in Nepal, India and Pakistan, and in parts of many others, especially rural areas, lack of staff (particularly female providers) has slowed the expansion of reproductive health services. In India and other countries, staff turnover is high and many positions remain vacant for long periods. In many countries, staff, particularly physicians, do not want to be posted in rural health facilities.

Situation Analysis findings show that staff can be trained to provide not only better quality family planning ser-vices, but other services to meet clients' reproductive and sexual health needs as well. Providers like the reproductive health approach, but question how many tasks an individual worker can be trained to carry out, particularly lower-level workers in health posts. In India, for example, an auxiliary nurse-midwife is already expected to do 40 tasks. How much more can she do?

Countries recognize that training is crucial to the success of the reproductive health approach. Peru, Mexico, Colombia and Jamaica have developed curricula for integrated training. In Bangladesh, a programme is being developed to train providers in all aspects of reproductive health. Romania has placed a priority on staff being trained in family planning in order to integrate it into primary health care. In general, however, training has not kept pace with the expansion of services.

In most countries, training curricula for both initial and in-service training are slowly being adapted to the client-centred, needs-based reproductive health approach, though sexuality, reproductive rights and the effects of gender relations on client-provider interactions are often missing or diluted. In all countries, it will take time to retrain all service providers, in addition to training new ones.

In training, as elsewhere, human resources are in short supply. There is a shortage of experts to redesign pre-service and in-service curricula and train the trainers. Decentralization of programme activities has shown how few staff are available to do training at the local level.

Training in reproductive health should begin in medical, nursing and midwifery courses. Pre-service training is generally less disruptive to the service delivery system, less expensive and more sustainable than in-service training,[48] but it calls for revising the curricula of medical schools and training institutions. Continued supervision and follow-up to training need to be strengthened in most countries.

To make the most of their training, providers need equipment and supplies, rewards, evaluation, opportunities to practice new skills, and better recruitment and job assignments.[49]

Monitoring and Evaluation

In order to maintain the gains (and highlight shortcomings) in policies and programmes that have emanated from the ICPD, the Programme of Action called for careful monitoring of implementation of the reproductive health and rights agenda. Ideally, programmes should have information systems that are simple and clear to use at the service delivery level; only the most essential data are collected; appropriate technology is applied; and findings are of immediate use at the service delivery level, but also at higher levels of the health-care system. Progress has been made in this area in many countries. For example, Iran as well as the state of Rajasthan in India offer examples of efficient national information system designs.

International organizations, including UNFPA, have taken the lead in developing reproductive health indicators to help countries revise their management information systems to monitor progress in implementing reproductive health and rights programmes. Most progress has been made in countries in which all stakeholders that can make use of the information (e.g., community representatives, service providers, programme managers, and researchers) have participated in designing the information systems.

For example, the Latin American and Caribbean Health Network — in collaboration with some governments in the region — has identified a set of thematic issues to monitor in each country they work in, including: reproductive health of adolescents; quality of care; management of unsafe abortion; male involvement; and the participation of women in decision-making. Qualitative and quantitative indicators have been identified for each of these issues that will be used to assess the reproductive health situation in each country.

NGOs, particularly women's groups, are also monitoring the implementation of the ICPD Programme of Action in order to hold governments accountable for the progress made. For example, the Latin American and Caribbean Women's Health Network is working in Brazil, Chile, Colombia, Nicaragua and Peru to monitor implementation. They are monitoring six issues: improving girls' status; male responsibility; participation of the women's health movement in decision-making processes; quality of reproductive health services; adolescents' access to sexual education and reproductive health services; and unsafe abortion.

Their monitoring has thus far revealed: great difficulties in including civil society and specifically women in the implementation process (in three of the five countries); an absence of data disaggregated by sex, age and geographical region; incomplete incorporation in all of the five countries of sexual and reproductive rights in laws and health services; continued poor quality of reproductive health services; no implementation of national sexual education programmes (in two of the five countries); and low impact of service and policy changes since Cairo on maternal mortality rates, with unsafe abortion still a principal cause of maternal death.[50]

Information and Care for Adolescents

Young women and men face many health risks, yet they receive inadequate information, guidance and services to help them negotiate the difficult passage to adulthood.

Adolescents need support to build self-esteem, to develop life skills, including managing intimate relationships, and to practise gender equality. Parents have the first responsibility: they need to be involved in the design of programmes for adolescents, and they should also be encouraged to talk to their children

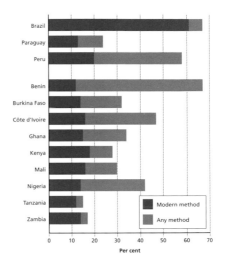

FIGURE 7: Percentage of Sexually Active, Never-Married Young Women, 15-19, Using Family Planning, Selected Countries

Source: B.S. Mensch, J. Bruce and M.E. Greene. 1998. *The Uncharted Passage: Girls' Adolescence in the Developing World.* New York: The Population Council.

about sexuality and reproductive health. Many studies have shown that better information encourages sexual responsibility among adolescents, including abstinence.[51]

In most cultures, gender norms produce a sexual double standard for girls and boys.[52] Girls often lack information or opportunities given to boys, though they are more at risk.[53] Early childbearing narrows the life opportunities of girls. In many countries, girls who become pregnant are not allowed to continue to attend school. In others, the education of boys is simply valued higher than that of girls: girls are two thirds of the more than 130 million children not attending school. In Kenya alone, an estimated 10,000 girls a year leave school because of pregnancy.[54]

BOX 18

Using Peer Education to
Reduce Adolescent Pregnancy

Pregnancy has become the principal cause of death among females between ages 15 and 19 in the Dominican Republic. Nearly one in four in this age group is either pregnant or has already given birth. There are few reproductive health services for young people in the marginal communities surrounding major cities, where 64 per cent of the population is concentrated.

Two non-governmental organizations — the Dominican Association for Family Well-being (*Profamilia*) and the Dominican Institute for Integrated Development (IDDI) — have been working since 1997 to expand young people's access to sexual education and reproductive health services in 36 neighbourhoods of Santo Domingo and in three smaller cities.

Using peer education and counselling, the UNFPA-supported project aims to reduce adolescent pregnancy and STD and AIDS infection rates by making young people more aware of the health risks of unprotected sex. Teens are encouraged to postpone their first sexual encounter or to maintain a faithful relationship with one partner.

Some 360 adolescents have been trained as voluntary peer counsellors on sexual and reproductive health matters. Each counsels between 15 to 30 youths and distributes educational material and, with parental consent, contraceptive methods (condoms, spermicides, and pills after their first prescription by a physician); they refer special cases to health services and follow up these referrals. The counsellors also conduct town meetings and theatrical presentations for their communities.

In two years, the project has counselled nearly 9,000 young people, 30 per cent of whom are not in school. Growing demand has given rise to open educational activities in schools, churches and community gathering places. Strong bonds of support have developed between counsellors and their clients, as became evident in the aftermath of the devastating Hurricane Georges.

The project has also trained 90 Ministry of Health physicians, nurses and psychologists in integrated adolescent health care, and produced a manual on sexual and reproductive health, a video and other educational materials.

In many countries, the topic of adolescent sexuality and reproductive health is still politically sensitive, and reproductive health information and services simply do not reach most adolescents. However, some 55 countries have taken policy and programme measures to address the health needs of adolescents including reproductive health. Some, such as Jamaica, are putting adolescents at the centre of their reproductive health strategies. Burkina Faso was one of the first West African countries to launch a reproductive health programme aimed at the needs of youth. The centrepiece of the programme has been the establishment of youth centres in urban areas offering reproductive health services and peer-based education.

Studies show that family life education should begin early, in some countries even before adolescence, to help young people through the years when they are reaching puberty, learning about their sexuality and beginning to be interested in sexual matters.[55]

Messages for sexually active youth should be different than for those who have not initiated sexual activity,[56] and should be as specific as possible. For example, in one study, Albanian youth said they want practical information such as how to avoid condom breakage and emergency contraception.[57]

Since unprotected sexual relations place adolescent girls at risk for unwanted pregnancy and both girls and boys at risk for STDs, including HIV/AIDS, they need not only preventive services, but also youth-friendly health services including diagnosis, treatment, information and counselling. Clinic staff need special training to treat young clients in a supportive and non-judgmental way.[58] Young adults also need information on family planning and on STDs including HIV/AIDS.

Worldwide experience[59] has shown that programmes for adolescents should:

- Recognize and address the fact that the programme needs of young people differ according to their sexual experience and other key characteristics.

- Start with what young people want and with what they are doing already to obtain reproductive health information and services.

- Include building skills (both generic and specific to reproductive health) as a core intervention.

- Engage adults in creating a safer and more supportive environment in which young people can develop and learn to manage their lives, including their sexual and reproductive health.

- Use a greater variety of settings and providers — both private and public, clinical and non-clinical — to provide sexual and reproductive health information and services.

- Make the most of what exists. Building upon and linking existing programmes and services in new and flexible ways so that they reach many more young people.

NGOs have been particularly active in testing new approaches to reaching adolescents, such as peer education, skills-building, counselling, and other services. Actions to foster understanding and support among adults in the family and in the community are now also recognized as a key investment. In Colombia, the NGO Profamilia, among many other reproductive health and women's empowerment activities, supports sexual and reproductive health education in youth centres in 20 of the country's cities.

In Kenya, the hit song "I Need to Know", performed by young Nairobi musicians, has helped adolescents ask that reproductive health be added to school health services. Through a youth-to-youth programme in the Marshall Islands, trained peer educators and counsellors provide health education to youth, their families and the community on issues such as teenage pregnancy, STDs and HIV/AIDS, substance abuse and nutrition. The programme also meets the contraceptive needs of adolescents.

Male Involvement and Responsibility

The ICPD Programme of Action recognizes that men need to take responsibility for their own sexual behaviour as well as respect and support the rights and health of their partners. Family planning programmes have generally ignored men, and have been designed to maintain gender norms dictating that reproduction and fertility control are women's responsibility.[60]

A study in Bolivia found that men were not as negative towards family planning as women thought. In fact, men's knowledge of family planning methods was slightly higher than women's, but couples did not always communicate about family size. In a study in Mali, the findings were not so positive: men in a focus-group discussion there were unanimous that women had no right to use family planning without their husbands' permission.[61]

While 36 countries reported measures to broaden or promote male involvement in sexual and reproductive health,[62] the situation in Nicaragua is fairly typical. That country's national health plan does not mention male responsibility for family planning and makes no provision for reproductive health services for men. In the Philippines, male reproductive health is one of the 10 components of the reproductive health package, but very little has been done so far. In Nepal, the programme is targeted primarily at women. Although the policy is for men and women to share the responsibility for family planning, the proportion of vasectomy acceptors, for example, has been steadily declining.

In Mexico, although providers generally understand the reproductive health concept, it continues to be seen as a "women's" programme. Little effort has been made to make the services more attractive to men or to involve men as partners.

In Morocco, married women of reproductive age are the main target and there is no clear strategy to address men. This is a serious problem in rural areas where some women may be best approached through their partners. To a large extent programme implementers and service providers in Uganda have ignored the role of men. Since the ICPD, some efforts are being made to reach men, including approaches aimed at addressing the effects of sociocultural attitudes and practices, as well as gender-based violence, on the sexual health and reproductive rights of Ugandan women and girls.

Among the countries that do have reproductive health activities for men, advocacy campaigns have been the most common activities. Since the ICPD, there appears to have been some increase in men's use of condoms and vasectomy and some expansion of male STD services.

In a few countries, NGOs especially are developing innovative approaches to support the involvement of males in pregnancy and childcare, and to encourage them to develop relationships based on equality and mutual respect. For example, in Mexico, a group of midwives have trained community health workers to teach men that pregnancy and birth is a family affair and not just "women's business".

An international "Men as Partners" Initiative is developing a reproductive

Teach Men about the Benefits of Family Planning

A prospective study of new contraceptive users in Mali, conducted as part of Family Health International's Women's Studies Project, has shown how important it is to involve men as partners in promoting reproductive health. Legally, Malian women do not need spousal consent to obtain contraception. However, husbands are statutory heads of the household, and their decisions about family planning use are critical to women's contraceptive practices. Programmes should therefore consider ways to educate men about the benefits of family planning, including the use of male peer education groups. In addition, policy makers may want to rethink laws that make the husband the final arbiter in decisions about women's health. For women whose husbands disapprove of family planning, providers should offer special counselling to help the woman resolve conflicts and make decisions that are best for them.

Source: B. Barnett and J. Stein. 1998. *Women's Voices, Women's Lives: The Impact of Family Planning.* Research Triangle Park, N.C.: Family Health International.

health curriculum to train providers and sensitize workers to the needs of men as clients.[63] Some countries have strengthened legislation that supports men's roles in the family, especially concerning child support.

Reproductive Health for Refugees and Displaced Persons

Ensuring the reproductive health of refugees and displaced persons, and protecting refugee women from sexual violence, are priority concerns wherever conflict or natural disaster takes place. The ICPD Programme of Action recognized the need to ensure reproductive rights and provide reproductive health care in emergency situations, particularly for women and adolescents.

The number of refugees, returnees and persons displaced within their own countries who fall under the mandate of the Office of the United Nations High Commissioner for Refugees (UNHCR) rose from 1.4 million in 1961 to a high of 27 million in 1995; it then fell to 22.3 million at the beginning of 1998.[64] Reproductive health care has been increasingly guaranteed in emergencies since the ICPD. Previously, reproductive health services had been largely ignored in refugee situations.

Reproductive health needs of women in emergency situations are being met as the result of an initiative by UNHCR and UNFPA, in collaboration with WHO, UNICEF, the International Federation of Red Cross and Red Crescent Societies, and various NGOs.[65] The initiative was launched in 1995 in response to the refugee crisis in Africa's Great Lakes region.

The programme trains staff and provides equipment and supplies to address needs in: family planning, including contraception; assisted childbirth; complications of unsafe abortions (post-abortion complications account for some 25-50 per cent of maternal deaths in refugee

BOX 20

Rape is Commonplace in Kenyan Refugee Camp

Thousands of Somalis have fled into Kenya to avoid fighting in their country. Now, in a UNHCR-run refugee camp housing 100,000 people near the small Kenyan town of Dadaab, they live in constant fear of being robbed, killed or raped by marauding bandits.

Five armed men raided the mud hut where Safia Wanderi, 34, was living with her husband and children. Three of the men — believed to be militiamen fighting in Somalia — took turns beating and raping her in front of her family. Safia's husband blamed her for the incident and abandoned the family.

Earlier, Safia says, her 11-year-old daughter was raped by a neighbour. She says many other women in Dadaab have had similar experiences.

More than 90 per cent of the rapes occur when women are collecting firewood from the outskirts of the camps. Rukim Nour Mohammed, 50, was raped and beaten one morning while collecting firewood and left to bleed to death. She managed to walk more than 15 kilometres back to the camp and find medical attention.

An aid worker at the camp, John Amollo, says traditional clan rivalries, heightened by the war, are a major reason why so many women are raped in Dadaab. "Whenever there is a conflict between clans, the worst punishment one clan can do to another is to rape their women." He says the problem is made worse because men in the camps are idle, frustrated and mentally traumatized by their experiences during the war.

Source: Voice of America, 18 May 1999.

situations); sexual violence and rape, including post-coital emergency contraception; and prevention of sexually transmitted diseases including HIV/AIDS.

A Reproductive Health for Refugees Consortium was established; it has produced needs assessment manuals and materials. An interagency working group developed a Minimum Initial Service Package, including essential drugs, supplies and basic surgical equipment. Emergency reproductive health kits have been stockpiled for distribution when needed.

UNFPA used these stockpiles in April 1999 to provide emergency reproductive health assistance to the hundreds of thousands of people fleeing the conflict in Kosovo to camps in Albania.[66] The Fund also undertook an investigation of sexual violence against Kosovar women; it uncovered alarming accounts of abduction, rape and torture. UNFPA and its partners are providing training for counsellors in offering support to refugees who have been subject to sexual violence.[67]

The plight of the Kosovars has attracted far more international attention than other ongoing refugee crises in Africa and Asia, where most of the world's 13 million refugees are found — the largest group are the 2.6 million Afghani refugees (1.2 million are in camps in Pakistan).[68]

Although reproductive health services are now being provided in emergencies, these efforts are often hampered by a lack of health personnel skilled in reproductive health information and services.

CHAPTER 4

Partnership and Empowerment

Mark Edwards / Still Pictures

The ICPD Programme of Action represents a consensus among governments, but it recognizes that giving practical effect to a concept of development centred on human aspirations and values will require collaboration among governments, civil society and the international community. Many of the issues were first brought to national and international attention by organizations outside government, and implementing its recommendations calls for action, advocacy, stewardship and feedback by many different participants.

In the forefront are health advocates, including family planning organizations, groups with an interest in education, women's organizations and those concerned with the family. Groups with a broader range of interests and concerns have also become involved, including many concerned with economic development, poverty, the environment, urban affairs, human rights, and religious and ethical questions. One of the most important signs of progress in implementing the Programme of Action in the last five years has been the growing involvement of organizations outside governments.

Photo: NGO community health worker shows women in Bangladesh village how to use a condom. Civil society groups are playing a growing role in carrying out the ICPD Programme of Action.

The Emerging Vision of Civil Society

This process has drawn renewed attention to the variety of and relationships among civil-society organizations and the public sector. Civil society takes different forms, but it may be thought of as a range of associations, organizations and institutions that bind people of similar interests together. It includes voluntary membership groups, the private sector and its groups and associations, cultural organizations and advocacy groups. Among its components are cooperatives, trade unions, micro-enterprise and self-help groups, women's groups, health and development advocacy and service groups, business associations, charitable organizations, religious bodies, trade unions, political parties, clans and other family-based systems, lobbying groups, social movements, political parties, professional associations, men's groups, youth groups — in short, the whole range of ways people get together to express their views and attain their ends other than through the formal State.[1]

The State can be involved, to different degrees in different settings, with a range of such groups (for example, as sponsor, partner, organizer, financier, manager, licenser or regulator), but the special roles and responsibilities of the State are distinct. The term non-governmental organization (NGO) is often used to refer to groups that are not part of the State apparatus but is generally understood to be less inclusive than civil-society organizations (CSOs) as a whole.[2]

NGOs and other civil society organizations have been active participants in assessing progress since the ICPD.

Parliamentarians play a special role in effecting national action. They are a bridge between civil society and the public sector, serving as the voice of local groups, leaders and other community influentials and of the electorate. Local leaders and respected individuals can also help to mobilize, mediate, and unify opinion and action.

National and international NGOs have been an important part of the ICPD process and its subsequent implementation and review. By the third Preparatory Committee meeting in 1994, which negotiated the final draft of the Programme of Action, 934 NGOs had been accredited. By the ICPD itself, 1,254 NGOs from 138 countries and territories had been accredited. They participated both directly (when they were included as members of country delegations) and indirectly (as advocates and as participants in the NGO Forum).

NGOs and other civil society organizations have also been active participants in assessing progress since the ICPD. A round-table meeting on partnership with civil society was held in Dhaka, Bangladesh, in July 1998.[3] There were also an NGO Forum and a Youth Forum at The Hague in February 1999, which attracted representatives from around the world.[4] NGOs active in the implementation of the Programme of Action were also accredited to participate in the preparatory meetings for the special session of the United Nations General Assembly in 1999.

In the years since the ICPD, the relationship between civil-society organizations and governments has continued to mature. In many countries, including many developing countries, NGOs have moved closer to involvement in decision-making. They are often included in discussion of national population policy and in official delegations to international and regional conferences. They are not only advocates for reproductive health and rights and gender equity but are also active in programmes to improve women's status and rights and reproductive health services.

The ICPD marked a turning point for recognition of NGOs as genuine partners of governments in planning, implementing, monitoring and evaluating policies and programmes. In the 1998 UNFPA field inquiry, however, only 49 of 114 countries reported having taken significant measures to promote the involvement of NGOs at various stages of policy and programme implementation.

A further 26 countries have taken significant measures to strengthen the institutional capacity of civil society. Some countries have undertaken both activities, so that a total of 56 countries have taken strong steps to strengthen the partnership with civil society. Nineteen countries have representatives of NGOs or other civil society members at the national bodies responsible for formulating policies or other committees to address issues of population and development and, more recently, reproductive health.

Nineteen countries have included NGOs in consultation and dialogue on policy and programme implementation. Eleven countries have established co-ordinating committees for NGO activities and 10 countries have created an enabling environment for civil society by establishing formal procedures for registration, providing tax incentives, or allowing broader funding mechanisms.

There has been significant progress, but five years after Cairo the partnership between governments and civil society is not complete or even, in some countries, acknowledged.

TABLE 1: Measures Taken to Develop Partnerships with Civil Society

Measures taken	Countries
Representation in government bodies	Belize, Botswana, Côte d'Ivoire, Egypt, Gambia, Ghana, Jamaica, Jordan, Lebanon, Madagascar, Morocco, Nepal, Peru, Senegal, Sri Lanka, Syria, Tunisia, Turkey
Consultation/dialogue	Bangladesh, Botswana, Colombia, Cuba, Dominican Republic, Gambia, Lao PDR, Latvia, Malawi, Maldives, Mali, Mexico, Mozambique, Panama, Swaziland, Tanzania, Trinidad and Tobago, Venezuela, Zambia
Coordination mechanism	Colombia, Côte d'Ivoire, Egypt, Gambia, Jamaica, Mali, Nepal, Romania, Senegal, South Africa, Sri Lanka
Creating enabling environment	Burundi, El Salvador, Guyana, Republic of Korea, Mexico, Nepal, Romania, Senegal, South Africa, Uganda
Recognition in policy/plan	Burkina Faso, Niger, Samoa, South Africa, Uruguay

Source: UNFPA. 1999. *Report of the 1998 UNPFA Field Inquiry: Progress in the Implementation of the ICPD Programme of Action.* New York: UNFPA.

The range of CSO and NGO activities throughout the world is too extended and diverse to be captured in any single report. The examples presented are only indicative.

Empowerment, Gender Equality and Reproductive Rights

Action for Women's Empowerment

The years since the ICPD have seen broad agreement on basic strategies to advance women's empowerment and participation, including the review of enabling conditions in law and social practice.

The principle of micro-credit loans for the poor, and especially for poor women, has been more widely recognized and supported by international donors and lenders (including international financial institutions), development assistance organizations, foundations and a growing number of nations.[5] Micro-credit approaches have been built into a diverse range of project activities advancing such concerns as reproductive health, environmental protection and education.

Women's social participation and activity in politics, through extension of the right to vote and through active candidacy, continues to increase in many settings. Some countries are reviewing their electoral laws, and some, such as Kuwait, have recently introduced the possibility of women as candidates in national and local elections. A growing number of countries, including India, the world's largest parliamentary democracy, are mandating a minimum presence of women in local and national elected bodies.

Debate continues among women's rights advocates about the strategies to be followed to advance women's empowerment and fuller partnership with men in social decision-making. The relative importance of advancing the power and voice given to individual women compared to advancing women's collective power through organizations and associations remains an issue.[6]

In Jordan, over 22 NGOs are involved in women's issues. Most of these NGOs educate women from low socioeconomic classes on their legal rights. In 1997 the Jordanian Women's Union established a hotline to provide women with legal counselling. Also in 1997, the United Nations Inter-agency Gender Task Force held a one-day workshop on the Convention on the Elimination of All Forms of Discrimination against Women, in Amman, opening doors for feminist groups like the National Jordanian Committee of Women's Rights to actively address inequities in the law.

This committee is working closely with all women's groups in dealing with constraints and difficulties women face because of the law. The committee meets frequently with the government to amend laws. For example, a significant recent change allows women to obtain a passport without consent from their father/ husband or legal guardian.[7]

Reproductive Health and Rights Advocacy

In many countries, a strong community for reproductive health and rights advocacy existed before Cairo (for example,

Bangladesh, Brazil, Chile, Colombia, India, Peru, the Philippines and South Africa). In some countries, it emerged or became stronger in preparation for Cairo (Egypt, Mexico, Malaysia and Nigeria), while in others it evolved after Cairo. In some countries the family planning community is a prominent advocate (in the Caribbean, for example) while in other countries, such as India, advocacy involves a broad range of development organizations.[8]

> In India, women's NGOs were instrumental in encouraging the Government to move away from targets and financial incentives.

Since the ICPD, NGOs, and particularly women's organizations, have continued their strong advocacy for reproductive health and rights.[9] NGOs in some countries have participated in the development of policy and legislative reforms. Many NGOs and civil society organizations have worked with their governments in advocacy campaigns to promote gender equality and equity, especially in female literacy and integrating males in reproductive health.[10]

In India, a number of vocal women's NGOs have influenced reproductive health policy. These groups were instrumental in raising issues of quality of care and client rights, and in encouraging the government to move away from method-specific targets and financial incentives.[11]

In South-east Asia, a women's group has produced a framework on reproductive rights from an Islamic perspective.

In Pakistan, the Family Planning Association of Pakistan has taken the lead in adopting the reproductive health approach and shifting to a life cycle approach. However, there is only one NGO working in the area of sexual health.[12]

In Ecuador, women's NGOs have been very active in advocating for reproductive health and reproductive rights issues and in ensuring that the empowerment of women and improved women's health, including reproductive health, would be included in the national social development agenda.[13]

Programmes in the Arab States region have undergone major changes in the post-ICPD period, particularly with UNFPA encouragement. There is now considerable involvement of NGOs in programme implementation on reproductive health and in related advocacy efforts on gender-based issues, including promotion of gender equality and equity, empowerment of women, male involvement concerns and adolescent reproductive health. The execution of country programme activities in the region by national NGOs has increased significantly since ICPD in Turkey, Jordan, Tunisia and Egypt. NGOs have participated in the assessment of national priorities and development of country programme activities.[14]

In Mexico and Brazil, an increasing number of NGOs are working with national and local governments to formulate, implement and evaluate reproductive health programmes that incorporate gender perspectives.[15]

Combating Gender-based Violence

Recent years have seen greater attention and heightened policy discussion of gender-based violence. An increasing number of countries have revised their criminal codes and police procedures to give greater protection to women who are subjected to violence in the home. Long-standing habits protecting men from review of their treatment of family members are being challenged in more countries. Women's self-help networks, at times with public assistance and support, are providing protection to victims of domestic abuse.

Increased attention has been given as well to exposing and advocating action on other acts of violence — including dowry murders, "honour" killings[16] and acid attacks.

In Pakistan, NGOs have recently established urban centres for victims of rape, incest and other forms of violence, and the Ministry of Women's Development is acknowledging the need to expand these services to rural areas.[17]

Model projects addressing gender and violence issues, including sexual abuse and domestic violence are being executed in Colombia and Ecuador, Cambodia and the Philippines; these projects involve link-ups between government agencies and law enforcement bodies, NGOs, and specialized women's groups, with funding and technical support provided by UNFPA.[18]

In Morocco, UNFPA is strengthening the collaboration between the NGO AMEP (Association maghrébine des études de population) and the Ministry of Justice through a project dealing with issues of marriage, divorce and violence against women. The project aims to strengthen the data collection system on marriage and divorce through training of judges and religious notaries, and to develop a monitoring mechanism for tracking violence against women.[19]

Strength in Numbers: Networks and Alliances

Networks and alliances of civil-society organizations to implement the ICPD Programme of Action have become increasingly important since Cairo. Networks of NGOs that advocate together can have a stronger voice than can individual organizations. Thus, to advance Cairo goals, groups have built broad alliances to overcome challenges to reproductive choice and freedom. South-South and North-South coalitions of women's health and rights organizations have also kept reproductive health and rights on the international agenda.[20]

Since ICPD, the number of NGOs working on reproductive health and rights has grown, as has the number of networks of civil society organizations. The 1998 UNFPA field inquiry found that of those countries reporting cases where civil society took major action, NGOs in about two thirds of the countries formed a coalition or a network under a common theme of women's rights, youth or reproductive health.

Countries in which coalitions have been formed include, among others, Botswana, Iran, Kenya, Madagascar, Nepal, El Salvador, Panama, Uzbekistan and the Cook Islands. The development of networks of NGOs to facilitate the implementation and follow-up of the ICPD Programme of Action has been particularly strong in the Latin American countries of Venezuela, Argentina, Uruguay, Peru, Chile, Mexico, Brazil and the Dominican Republic.[21]

In Asia, a special initiative has taken shape through the collaborative efforts of the Commission of the European

Communities (EC), UNFPA and some 22 European NGOs and 66 national organizations and institutions. The EC/UNFPA Initiative for Reproductive Health in Asia targets seven countries in South Asia and South-east Asia, to help provide quality reproductive health services to hard-to-reach communities and address the reproductive health needs of adolescents. Over $30 million will be spent during a three-year period (1998-2001) through 43 separate projects in Bangladesh, Cambodia, Laos, Nepal, Pakistan, Sri Lanka and Viet Nam. An important aspect of the EC/UNFPA Initiative for Reproductive Health in Asia is capacity building of community-based organizations, and promoting linkages among NGOs, and between NGOs and government services.

The Turkish Family Planning Association is developing a network of NGOs which will have the capacity to advocate for the implementation of ICPD and Beijing action programmes among national and local policy makers.[22]

In the Arab States, a UNFPA project to strengthen the capacity of NGOs improved management capacity of around 162 NGOs in 18 countries. It also facilitated NGO networking at the regional level and increased governmental and public awareness about the NGO sector and its roles, problems and needs.[23]

The Argentinean experience shows how alliances between health professionals, community members and churches can work in an environment with diverse cultural concerns. Reproductive health services were introduced in 1998 without opposition of any kind in the province of Buenos Aires, which has a third of the country's population. A law endorsing creation of a family planning programme for women was also the result of such alliances.[24]

Mexico's Grupo de Información en Reproducción Elegida (GIRE, the Information Group on Reproductive Choice), founded in 1992, participates in several groups that were created to help monitor the government's actions to implement the ICPD Programme of Action. In addition, the National Forum of Women and Population Policy, a non-governmental network of over 70 institutions nationwide, is designing mechanisms for the promotion of these accords.[25]

Since 1996, the Latin American and Caribbean Women's Health Network has been working in Brazil, Chile, Colombia, Nicaragua and Peru on monitoring ICPD implementation. Additional countries are considering similar initiatives. This multi-country effort, actively brokered and supported by UNFPA, embodies the basic principles of social accountability contained in the Programme of Action. It is forging partnerships (tripartite commissions, or other institutional arrangements) in which government, local NGOs (particularly women's groups, health advocates and national researchers) and United Nations organizations and other donors will collaborate in regular and long-term monitoring.

Their research has revealed uneven progress to date, including incomplete incorporation of sexual and reproductive rights in laws and health services and the continued need to improve the quality of reproductive health services. Of special concern, they have noted the low impact of service and policy changes since Cairo on maternal mortality and the continued role of unsafe abortion as a principal cause of maternal death.[26]

Governments and Civil Society in Partnership

NGOs have collaborated with governments to establish institutional mechanisms for women's rights. There are new ministries for women in Colombia, Costa Rica and Mali. China, Fiji, Iran, Mali and Nigeria have launched women's action plans stemming from both the Cairo and Beijing conferences. Government and NGOs in Zimbabwe have begun national consultations on a new gender policy.[27]

NGO networks have kept reproductive health and rights on national and international agendas.

In Ghana, NGOs and civil-society organizations are taking participatory roles in policy development. The highest government body responsible for coordinating population issues in Ghana, the National Population Council, has NGO representation. NGOs have also been involved in developing Ghana's Reproductive Health Policy and Service Standards document. In Botswana and Tanzania, women's activists have worked with government bodies to bring about stiffer penalties for rape, especially for rapists who are found to be HIV-positive.[28]

In the Philippines, the National Commission on the Role of Filipino Women in collaboration with eight civil society organizations and NGO networks organized the Cairo-Copenhagen-Beijing Interface Conference to continue to conduct forums to advance government programmes regarding the Programme of Action objectives. In Morocco, the National Population Commission, established in 1998, carries out coordinated advocacy with NGOs.[29]

In Mexico, the National Forum of Women and Population Policy, a network of 70 Mexican women's NGOs and academic institutions, has worked to improve relations with the government through its partnership efforts. The concept of partnership formalized in the ICPD Programme of Action posed a challenge to the Mexican feminist movement, which was not accustomed to negotiating with government officials. In addition, deep mistrust existed on both sides. Since then, there has been a clear movement towards partnerships in which NGOs share responsibility with government institutions for implementing the Cairo accords.[30]

In South-east Asia, the Asian-Pacific Resource and Research Centre for Women and the Asian and Pacific Development Centre conducted an eight-country study in 1996 of the environment for implementation of the ICPD Programme of Action. In China, Fiji, Indonesia, Malaysia, Pakistan, Singapore, Thailand and Viet Nam they found that the environment for NGOs remains problematic with government agencies particularly sensitive about policy advocacy-oriented NGOs. Few NGOs undertook advocacy activities. The capacity of women's NGOs to play an effective policy advocacy role was not strong.[31]

The Government of Peru has introduced new procedures to ensure that sterilizations are carried out only with full consent. A Tripartite Commission for follow-up of the implementation of the ICPD Programme of Action was established in August 1997, in response to allegations by women's NGOs and others that the Ministry of Health was providing voluntary surgical sterilization with insufficient counselling. NGOs, universities, international cooperation agencies and government institutions are represented; leadership rotates among these groups.

After reviewing the programme, the Commission concluded that the criticism was greatly exaggerated, but that there were problems with the quality of services. Since March 1998, the Ministry has strengthened counselling procedures, introduced mandatory waiting times before performing sterilizations, and standardized the accreditation of service providers and facilities. In April 1999, Costa Rica created its own Tripartite Commission following the Peruvian model; similar efforts are under way in Chile and elsewhere in the region.

The Canadian International Development Agency and other donors support capacity strengthening of civil-society organizations to promote gender equality.[32] A study of 10 member States of the Development Assistance Committee of the Organization for Economic Cooperation and Development (OECD/DAC) found that some have not engaged with local women's organizations in any significant way, whereas others have supported such organizations to work on sensitive issues such as female genital mutilation, abortion and violence against women.[33]

UNFPA is currently supporting the development of an Arab Support Centre for NGOs to promote networking, cooperation and coordination among them, and contribute to NGO capacity building.[34] International assistance, through projects such as the Policy Project of the Futures Group International (funded by the United States Agency for International Development) and the Access Project of the Centre for Development and Population Activities (CEDPA, supported by UNFPA, the World Bank, UNICEF, USAID and nearly 30 foundations) have helped NGOs improve their advocacy and service efforts.[35]

The Policy Project is working with 13 networks in eight countries to strengthen women's capacity to engage in policy dialogue and to expand the capability of the networks for advocacy, training and research. In Jordan, for example, in addition to providing advocacy training to a number of women's organizations, the project helped carry out a national workshop to set priorities for research on women's issues. The first study focused on women's participation in the 1997 general election as candidates and voters.

In South Africa, the NGO Women's Health Project worked with three provincial governments to transform reproductive health services. In addition to improving quality of care, the project sought to increase understanding of the impact of social inequality, especially gender inequality, on health and health services.

Governments are sometimes inflexible in their programme design and implementation; partnership with an NGO can make flexibility and innovation possible. Room exists for NGOs to help

In Mexico, a network of women's NGOs has worked to build a partnership with government institutions.

shape the agendas of governments. However, success depends on setting up partnerships that are mutually supportive, managing existing partnerships effectively, and getting government officials at all levels to support the ideas and the process.[36]

Collaboration with Other Sectors of Civil Society

Renewed efforts have been made since the ICPD to mobilize the efforts of religious and cultural groups, parliamentarians and the private sector for the implementation of the Programme of Action.

Religious Leaders

Many religious leaders can play an important role in promoting population and reproductive health issues and as an important partner in the ICPD Programme of Action implementation given their strong authority and the influence that they have on their constituents.

UNFPA has recognized this and involved religious authorities in relevant discussions. The Fund's Africa Division organized an international conference on Islam and Population in November 1998 in Niamey, Niger, for over 80 Muslim leaders and scholars from 19 sub-Saharan African countries and eight other countries. The meeting made recommendations to further the implementation of the ICPD Programme of Action especially with regard to Islam and reproductive health, the status of women, and population and development.

Religious leaders are also increasingly involved in country-level activities. In Ghana, for example, eight religious

organizations are currently preparing manuals to incorporate population/family life education into religious activities and to encourage parents to discuss sexuality with their children.

In Uganda, for example, the Population Secretariat coordinates and oversees the implementation of advocacy activities and provision of reproductive health services of a national consortium of NGOs where Catholic and Muslim leaders are represented.

Parliamentarians United for Reproductive Health and Rights

Parliamentarians play a unique role in the government-civil society partnership. They are in essence the bridges between civil society and governments. Parliamentarians can play a direct role in defining programmes and allocating budgets. Significant progress at the advocacy level has sensitized parliamentarians to ICPD issues. As a result, the parliamentary movement has grown, its intra-parliamentary lobbying activities have increased and legislation has been promulgated, and regional and international parliamentarians' networks are thriving.

Parliamentary advocacy has enabled the level of funding to be maintained and sustained in some countries where such funding was to be decreased or eliminated. For example, in the Asia and Pacific Region, UNFPA funded two projects which organized conferences and forums involving parliamentarians.

Over 200 parliamentarians representing 103 countries took part in a three-day international forum as part of the ICPD+5 meetings at The Hague in February 1999. They agreed to a declaration calling for legislation, advocacy

UNFPA and Parliamentarians

UNFPA has been working with parliamentarians since its inception in 1969.

In 1979 UNFPA arranged an International Organization of Parliamentarians on Population and Development meeting in Colombo, Sri Lanka. The Fund organized a subsequent series of meetings of Asian parliamentarians, including a meeting in Beijing in 1982 that facilitated the formation of the Asian Forum of Parliamentarians on Population and Development.

Additional support has been given in recent years to other regional groups of parliamentarians, including the Inter-American Group of Parliamentarians on Population and Development and the Forum of African and Arab Parliamentarians on Population and Development.

These regional groups were instrumental in organizing the International Forum of Parliamentarians on ICPD Review in The Hague in February 1999.

and increased resources to ensure that governments meet their ICPD obligations with respect to reproductive health and rights, gender equity and empowerment of women, and prevention of violence against women, including FGM.[37]

The Private Sector

The private sector has the potential to play several important roles in the implementation of the Programme of Action. First, businesses with direct interests in the provision of supplies, services and technical know-how can work with governments to eliminate barriers to access to services and information and to development of markets for those able to pay. They can work to develop mutually rewarding agreements for expansion of service and logistical networks.

Second, they can act to ensure that family planning and reproductive health services are included in the packages of benefits and services that are offered to their employees and in the regulatory frameworks governing enterprises.

Providing workers with information and education on family life issues has for years been a goal of UNFPA collaboration with the International Labour Organization. The direct benefits to participating enterprises include productivity increases from reduction of illnesses of employees and their families and less stressful family lives. Recently in Cameroon, Eritrea and Malawi, for example, UNFPA has provided support to the Ministries of Labour in order to provide family life education for workers in public and private enterprises as well as reproductive health services through health centres or community-based initiatives.

The Tata Corporation in India, a large industrial firm, has advanced the implementation of the Programme of Action with special reference to the reproductive health of adults, a focus on youth, and attention to the prevention of HIV/AIDS. The Tata Group has experimented boldly with different approaches. It formed partnerships with mothers-in-law, whose support was needed to enable young women to go for health care or attend family planning clinics. It held consultations and helped initiate community-based clinics run by youth clubs and voluntary organizations.

4

BOX 22

Involving the Private Sector in Meeting Contraceptive Commodity Needs

Under its Global Initiative on Reproductive Health Commodity Management, UNFPA is helping countries determine how to meet their contraceptive and reproductive health commodity requirements for the next 10 years. The initiative provides technical assistance to estimate national needs and develop strategies to meet them. It also helps to facilitate negotiations between governments and commodity suppliers, and brings experts from different countries together to compare and contrast their needs and approaches. An advisory group including major donors meets periodically, contributing to better coordination of commodity provision.

A major aim is to increase private sector and NGO involvement in making affordably priced products and services more accessible, freeing public resources to serve groups that cannot afford to pay full price for them.

As part of its national programme in India, UNFPA has organized meetings with private-sector producers and distributors to improve the availability of temporary methods of contraception. The intent is to provide more choices to those seeking to space their pregnancies.

Source: UNFPA. 1999. *Donor Support for Contraceptive Commodities 1997.*

Business associations and community groups also have a role to play. Rotary International has used its network to provide a platform to promote greater awareness of population and development issues locally. Some national clubs have mobilized resources for population activities, often with support from partner Rotarians in other countries, the Rotary Foundation and bilateral donors. The Rotarians are encouraging community programmes for the reduction of population pressures, prevention of environmental degradation and elimination of poverty.

Rotary International established the Rotary International Fellowship on Population and Development in Senegal in 1995 and has expanded activities to other interested national associations. It is now the largest fellowship within Rotary International.

In Thailand, the Business Coalition for AIDS consists of 126 enterprises that provide in-kind assistance to initiatives to combat the pandemic.

Medical Associations

Medical associations, such as the Commonwealth Medical Association and the International Federation of Obstetricians and Gynecologists, and their local affiliates, have advocated for expanded access to quality reproductive health services. These organizations also assist WHO, UNFPA, UNICEF and other international agencies in defining national and international codes of conduct and standards of care that protect basic rights. They can also play important roles in formulating the broader health policy context in which reproductive health services are offered.

Strengthening Partnerships

Current Constraints

The need for political will and resources. While governments have increasingly included NGOs in the population programme process, such inclusion has often been primarily of NGOs as part of the government-directed programme. While the ICPD mandates working with women's organizations and other NGOs, some of the relationships that have been developed are contracts for service by governments to NGOs. These relationships tend to favour NGOs specialized in family planning and in some cases other reproductive health services. In many countries there has been a relative lack of commitment and financial resources to support NGOs that work for long-term empowerment, gender equity and social change through community mobilization, advocacy and political action across sectors.[38]

Incomplete partnerships in the programme planning phase. Furthermore, donor organizations, although they promote participation and partnership, have not been consistently successful in supporting civil-society organizations and NGOs in the policy development and programme implementation process. The study of the OECD/DAC's 10 member organizations found that although all organizations emphasize building partnerships and stakeholder consultation and participation, policy dialogues still tend to be limited primarily to the donors and the counterpart governments. Civil society groups in general and women's organizations in particular are often marginalized to the process of consultation and dialogue.[39]

Lack of shared understandings of partnership. Many NGOs, therefore, perceive that their "participation" with governments in the implementation of the ICPD Programme of Action needs to be better realized. NGOs have often been invited to participate in ongoing programmes without having the ability to design or reorient the programmes. Some NGOs feel they are viewed as tools for implementing established programmes rather than as partners who can play a valuable role through dialogue and advocacy.[40]

The need for coordination. Little coordination exists among the reproductive health programmes directed by governments, NGOs and the private sector; these programmes operate separately and in parallel.

Other constraints include: a lack of sufficient financial resources, insufficient NGO and government institutional capacity, human resources and trained staff; insufficient NGO coordination; an insufficiently trusting government-NGO relationship; a lack of awareness or understanding of the issues by the civil society; a lack of awareness or understanding of the importance of partnership; and weak political commitment.

Providing reliable financing

One suggestion that has been repeated in consultations calls on governments to earmark a core grant to support NGO/civil society involvement, and on international aid agencies to set aside a percentage of country programme funds for NGO and civil society participation.

In Chad, for example, the Government used World Bank International Development Assistance to create a special multimillion-dollar fund to assist

4

NGOs working in the population field. In Gabon, a national network of youth NGOs was established through assistance from UNFPA. The powerful Catholic Federation of Youth Movements is a member of this network. In the Gambia, the Government allocated funds and other resources to various NGOs to implement programmes in advocacy and reproductive health, sexual health and family planning.

In a UNFPA-supported project in India, 10 per cent of the project funds will be programmed through NGOs. In a UNFPA-supported programme in the Philippines, approximately 25 per cent of funds earmarked for reproductive health services were programmed through NGOs.

Progress has been limited in improving NGOs' financial sustainability, transparency and responsiveness to constituencies.

Strengthening institutional capacity

In at least 44 countries, NGOs have taken initiatives in strengthening their institutional sustainability, building coalitions or mobilizing resources. Overall, however, in most countries, NGOs have achieved only limited progress towards strengthening their institutional financial sustainability, networking, and improving their transparency, accountability and responsiveness to constituencies or to mobilizing additional public and financial support for population activities.

Mechanisms to promote and strengthen the enhanced professionalism of civil society institutions might include, for example, the establishment of training and research centres to build the managerial skills and organizational capacities of NGOs; and the creation of an independent body to accredit NGOs and to set standards for NGO operations.

UNFPA and NGOs

Since the ICPD, UNFPA has been actively endeavouring to promote and enhance cooperation between NGOs, governments and the international community.

The Fund established the Non-Governmental Organization Advisory Committee to UNFPA to promote cooperation with the NGO community. Discussions have addressed issues needing special attention such as male responsibility and participation, quality of care, violence against women and harmful social practices. In the annual meetings held since 1995, the committee has made numerous recommendations directed to UNFPA for action at international and national levels, to the NGOs themselves, and to governments and the donor community.[41]

In 1997 UNFPA and the Women's Environment and Development Organization cooperated in advocacy efforts to promote gender equality and equity and the empowerment of women as well as in identifying 25 national and community-based women's NGOs worldwide for disbursement of one-time capacity-building grants.[42]

UNFPA has expanded its use of NGOs as executing agencies for its projects and programmes.[43] The Fund increased its expenditures directed through NGOs by 77 per cent in absolute terms during the period 1995-

1998 compared to 1991-1994 (from $92 million to $163 million). Fully 132 NGOs have been accredited as potential executing agencies for UNFPA-funded interregional or regional projects.

In December 1996, UNFPA organized, in collaboration with the Office of the United Nations High Commissioner for Human Rights (UNHCHR) /United Nations Centre for Human Rights and the United Nations Division for the Advancement of Women (DAW), the Round Table of Human Rights Treaty Bodies on "Human Rights Approaches to Women's Health, with a Focus on Reproductive and Sexual Health and Rights." Held in Glen Cove,

New York, this meeting constituted the first time that experts from all six treaty bodies, representatives of the United Nations system entities and NGOs had met together to discuss a substantive area.

Participants examined the interpretation of human rights treaties, and explored the need for new procedures and indicators to promote and monitor reproductive and sexual health-related rights. A major outcome of the round table was a call for treaty bodies, United Nations agencies and NGOs to work together to integrate a gender-sensitive reproductive rights/human rights perspective in their respective programmes.

4

BOX 23

Enabling Environment for Effective Partnership

In 1998, UNFPA and the United Nations Population Division organized a round table meeting on partnership with civil society to implement the ICPD Programme of Action. The meeting recommended that all governments facilitate the involvement of civil society in formulating, implementing, monitoring and evaluating policies, strategies and programmes, by:

• Creating common forums for dialogue;

• Re-examining concepts, assumptions, agendas, priorities;

• Listening to and respecting the experiences of other partners;

• Identifying and building on the comparative strengths of various partners and utilizing existing relationships;

• Identifying key issues, players and institutions;

• Developing mutual accountability and transparency among partners;

• Developing joint plans of action at various levels;

• Strengthening capacities at all levels and ensuring sustainability;

• Encouraging coalition-building and networking;

• Continuing to monitor the implementation of the Programme of Action.

Source: UNFPA. 1998. Partnership with Civil Society to Implement the Programme of Action, International Conference on Population and Development. Round Table Meeting. Dhaka, Bangladesh, 27-30 July 1998.

In collaboration with DAW, UNHCHR, the United Nations Development Fund for Women (UNIFEM), and the Committee on the Elimination of Discrimination against Women (CEDAW), UNFPA is supporting efforts to implement the recommendations of the Glen Cove meeting. Activities include: training UNFPA staff, governments and NGOs in reproductive rights within a human rights framework; involving CEDAW experts in UNFPA programming processes; cooperating with governments, NGOs and the treaty bodies to strengthen mechanisms for the reporting process to CEDAW by States parties; and organizing advocacy seminars.[44] UNFPA field offices have been encouraged to assist NGOs involved in preparing shadow reports for CEDAW on eliminating discrimination against women in access to sexual and reproductive health services.

In 1997, UNFPA joined UNIFEM and others in a Latin America-wide United Nations Campaign against Violence against Women, inspired by women's rights activists who have long voiced the need to address gender violence. The campaign is expected to institutionalize partnerships among governments, women's groups and NGOs, universities, medical professions, students, the media, police, religious groups and United Nations organizations.[45]

UNFPA has also played an active role in promoting greater coordination of United Nations programme development in collaboration with other agencies, donors, governments and CSOs. The Executive Director has been Chair of the Task Force on Basic Social Services for All. The Task Force has distributed guidelines for use by United Nations Resident Coordinators in assisting the formulation of national plans for development. The Fund is also involved in developing the United Nations Development Assistance Framework, which seeks to reduce duplication, allocate tasks according to capabilities and comparative advantages, and involve all stakeholders, including CSOs, in development efforts.

CHAPTER 5

Finding the Resources

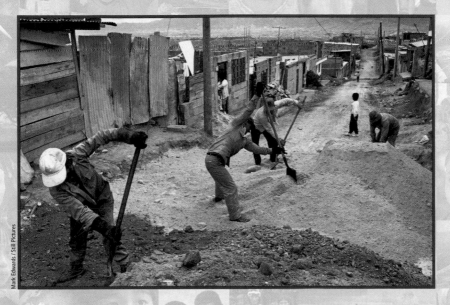

Mark Edwards / Still Pictures

Investing in Development

Thirty years after UNFPA started its operations with $1 million, global resources for population and development are reckoned in billions of dollars. Five years after the historic consensus of the ICPD, its goals are universally accepted as necessary to promote human rights and personal well-being, fight poverty and improve national and global security.

The integrated package of population and reproductive health investments in developing countries defined in the ICPD Programme of Action, costed at $17 billion in 2000, is recognized as a vital part of overall development strategy.

A complete social services package would add basic health, basic education, nutrition, and low-cost water and sanitation in less-developed regions. The yearly cost of the total package has been estimated in the range of $30-40 billion above 1990 levels in the year 2000.[1]

Photo: Workers repair road in poor barrio in Bogotá, Colombia. Increased resources for development are essential to alleviating poverty and improving people's quality of life.

Coming up short

The world is far from meeting these needs. Official development assistance for *all* purposes, economic as well as social, has shrunk from almost $61 billion in 1992 to $47.6 billion in 1997. Meanwhile the demands of peace-keeping and emergencies have increased dramatically.

Funding for the ICPD Programme of Action is far behind the total foreseen for the end of the century. Both donor and programme countries will fall short of their estimated shares of the burden ($5.7 billion and $11.3 billion, respectively). The donor countries are providing only about $1.9-2.0 billion. A small number of large developing countries account for most of the $7.7 billion annually from domestic resources.

Donors are providing $1.9 billion a year — one third of the $5.7 billion needed to implement the ICPD agenda.

The private sector, including NGOs and foundations, is helping to bridge the assistance gap, and user fees for services are generating resources in developing countries — but nothing can replace the inherent responsibility of governments, both developing and donor. Most people in most countries depend to some extent on public education and health care; and poor people in poor countries depend on them more than most.

The Resource Challenge

The shortage of resources is not confined to population. It has structural as well as temporary causes, such as:

- The pressures of globalization;

- A widening gap between wealthy and poor nations;

- A widening gap between rich and poor within nations;

- Donors' retreat from political commitment to development assistance.

In addition, developing countries have had to weather financial and economic crises, and sweeping "structural adjustment" of their economies emphasizing reductions in public expenditure.

Structural adjustment programmes are intended to improve countries' potential for economic development by reducing public sector expenditure. But structural adjustment has had a disproportionate impact on the poor, who depend most on free or low-cost public services. When public services are cut or charges for service are imposed the poor have nowhere to turn. This has been documented in education and health as well as other areas.[2]

All of these have had their effect on implementing the ICPD Programme of Action.

What will it take?

Finding the resources to move the ICPD Programme of Action from paper to practice is a matter of political commitment as well as of money. It calls for additional investment in reorganization and reform in the public sector, and in recruitment, training and motivation to make the most of human resources. It calls for:

- Renewed efforts to **increase resources overall**, which were made by all countries at the International Conference on Population and Development;

- Renewed dedication to provide an **increased share of available resources,** international, public and private, to basic social services including reproductive health;

- **Efficiency gains.** A variety of actions can produce gains in efficiency, depending on local conditions;

- **Partnerships** between governments, civil society and donors — to improve financing and extend information and services to where they are most needed.

This is a challenge as much for the international community as for countries, both to find additional assistance for development, and to direct it in the most productive way.

Increasing Resources

Developing countries are engaged in three simultaneous transitions: changing the definition of essential health services and the ways they are integrated with each other; redistributing responsibilities in public service systems from central to local actors; and redefining the role and scope of public services.

Increased external resources for population and reproductive health programmes are essential to help countries make these transitions, and at the same time take advantage of them to implement the recommendations of ICPD, for example:

- To design and implement programmes which respond fully to clients' needs and priorities in the changing environment;

5

BOX 24

Debt Relief and the Resource Challenge

To add to their problems, many poorer countries are saddled with extremely high levels of external debt, accumulated with the encouragement of the lending institutions before the importance of basic social investments was appreciated. In some countries, debt service is several times the total national allocations to health or education.

A helping hand

One new mechanism to reduce debt burdens is to exchange debt for increased social investment. Uganda has negotiated a "debt swap" with international financial institutions, and other countries are discussing the possibilities. Uganda's savings have largely been used to eliminate fees for primary school. In two years enrolment jumped from 54 to 90 per cent, in marked contrast to other heavily indebted countries.

Donors have forgiven some of their bilateral debt as a response to natural disasters in Central America. Expansion of the debt relief programme of the World Bank and the International Monetary Fund (the Highly Indebted Poor Countries initiative) has been proposed by donor countries. The five year review of ICPD implementation urged further exploration.

External assistance is critical to the ICPD agenda, including promotion of male responsibility with respect to reproductive health and the family. Above, father and child in Egypt.

- To help strengthen physical, human resource and institutional infrastructures;

- To provide technical assistance and commodities.

Additional external and national resources are urgently required:

- To expand advocacy for the necessary investments for development;

- To improve data for programme design, implementation and monitoring;

- To meet the growing volume and diversity of service demands and needs;

- To improve the quality of health services, including for sexual and reproductive health;

- To retrain staff to eliminate provider-based barriers to voluntary service access, including poverty status, geographical location, gender, age, and ethnic or cultural group;

- To extend information and services to underserved populations, particularly the poor;

- To address the cultural, social and economic barriers that restrict information and opportunity;

- To improve the recruitment, the training, the retention and the motivation of the staff needed to implement the programmes, from the central to the local levels.

Where Does the Money Come from Now?

Estimates of global, regional and domestic resource flows for population and development programmes, including reproductive health, are based on information for countries and institutions reporting in 1997.[3]

External Assistance

Donors are providing about $1.9-2.0 billion per year. Leading donors in the 1990s such as the Netherlands, Norway and Denmark have allocated a relatively large share of their GNP to development assistance including the share to population; others, notably Australia, Finland and the United Kingdom, have begun to increase the population share. On the other hand, the United States, while still the leading donor for population ac-

UNICEF / 1044 / Nicole Toutounji

tivities, has recently reduced its level of support.

Japan, UNFPA's largest contributor since 1986, has fulfilled its pledge for international assistance in global population-related issues for the period 1994-2000.

The European Commission/UNFPA project for reproductive health projects in Asia (see pages 76-77) is an example of the will of EC members to fulfil the commitment they declared prior to the ICPD. But much still needs to be done to streamline the process for moving EC population funds through its bureaucracy.

Prospects for increased donor support include further development of the 20/20 Initiative. This is a mutual commitment between developed and developing country partners to allocate, on average, 20 per cent of their official development assistance (ODA) and 20 per cent of their national budgets, respectively, to basic social services. The five components of basic social services, in a definition agreed on at a 20/20 Initiative meeting in Oslo in 1996, are basic health; basic education; reproductive health, including family planning and sexual health; nutrition; and basic water and sanitation.[4]

The World Bank is mobilizing resources for basic social services, including reproductive health, for example, by taking measures to address the debt burden of highly indebted poor countries. It has also provided $3.6 billion to help the poor cope with economic hardships and change, and to assist refugees and people displaced by emergencies.

The World Bank also provides loans for health, nutrition, and population; for education; and for the social protection components of other loans ($8.48 billion in 1998). Bank lending has increasingly supported integrated reproductive health programmes, both directly and through sector-wide assistance and health reform.

Donations by foundations are becoming more important. The Ford Foundation, the Rockefeller Foundation, the MacArthur Foundation, the Hewlett Foundation and the Mellon Foundation[5] each contributed between $10 million and $30 million for population activities in 1996 and similar amounts in 1997. The Packard Foundation announced in November 1998 that it will allocate more than $300 million to international population and reproductive health programmes over the next five years.

In its first year of grants, the United Nations Foundation, set up with $1 billion by Ted Turner in 1997, gave over $12 million to various reproductive health and women's empowerment projects, including several for adolescent reproductive and sexual health.

The William H. Gates Foundation, which supports efforts to improve global health and education, has contributed $1.7 million to the United Nations, for specific use by UNFPA to support collaboration among developing countries. This year it provided a multi-year $50 million grant to the Columbia University School of Public Health to combat maternal mortality, traditionally the most difficult of all reproductive health problems to solve. Another $20 million dollars has been earmarked to support Johns Hopkins University to train developing country professionals in reproductive health. In June 1999, Bill and Melinda Gates added $5 billion to the Foundation's endowment, doubling the funds available.

5

Domestic Resources

Globally, it is estimated that in 1997 governments and national NGOs spent almost $7 billion on population programmes from resources mobilized in developing countries.[6] It is further estimated, with considerably less precision, that private channels in these countries were responsible for another $1 billion.

It is extremely difficult, however, to establish exactly what is being spent on implementing the population and reproductive health package of the Programme of Action.[7] Accounting systems measure general categories of inputs such as salaries and supplies rather than services provided. The ICPD package costs only services delivered through primary health care, not hospital care or other services needed at higher levels of the system.

More important, out-of-pocket expenditures by individuals are difficult to monitor. Not all countries survey household expenditures, and surveys do not usually inquire about specific health services. There is a growing body of information about payments for family planning and maternal and child health services[8] but this does not address other reproductive health outlays.

Programme countries in Asia and the Pacific mobilized the most for population and reproductive health programmes in their countries (over $5 billion), followed by Latin America and the Caribbean (over $1 billion). Smaller amounts were mobilized in Western Asia, North Africa and sub-Saharan Africa. Over $100 million is estimated to have been mobilized in countries in economic transition.

A small number of large countries accounted for most of this: the com-

Mark Edwards / Still Pictures

Basic social services such as education have been hurt by a scarcity of resources caused in part by the decline in development assistance. Above, village school in India.

bined expenditures of China, India, Indonesia, the Islamic Republic of Iran and Mexico amounted to $5.5 billion, approximately 80 per cent of all domestic resources for reproductive health and family planning services. Most other developing countries, and particularly the 51 least-developed countries, had neither the public resources nor private income to meet their domestic needs.

In some areas, the impact of funding shortfalls is already apparent. The ICPD Programme of Action proposed $1.3 billion for STD/HIV/AIDS-prevention programmes in the year 2000, compared with recent levels of less than $550 million yearly.[9] Prevention programmes are the most cost-effective strategy to reverse the pandemic.[10] Additional resources, not part of the ICPD estimates, will be needed for the care of individuals infected with HIV/AIDS and to help families, communities and countries affected.

Many countries are trying to increase the contributions of the private sector and non-governmental organizations. More than 37 countries had private-sector initiatives (most often the commercial marketing of subsidized contraceptives) before 1994 and nine more have begun since the ICPD. Some countries, such as Bolivia and Mexico, now include reproductive health services in national insurance schemes. Despite many technical and managerial challenges, especially reaching poor and other marginalized populations, private-sector involvement will probably increase. A private-sector initiative co-sponsored by UNFPA encourages private-sector inter-

est and partnership to meet reproductive health needs.

Increasing Efficiency

Reaching high efficiency requires high initial investments, to pay both for current services and for improving them.

Health-sector reform, for example, will pay substantial dividends, but the costs of transition should not be underestimated.

Efficiency cannot be seen in isolation. Advocacy, for example, is efficient in stimulating demand for services; but the services must then improve to meet demand. Referral is an efficient way to supplement clinic services, but only if the referral points are well-placed and equipped to handle the additional load.

Investments often set the stage for later efficiency gains. Industrial countries brought maternal mortality down to today's very low levels by equipping more institutions to handle all kinds of emergencies, including obstetric emergencies. Some investments which appear to be inefficient produce gains later, such as monitoring the self-medication of all tuberculosis patients. The initial investment stimulated development of more cost-effective methods of ensuring compliance.

When efficiency considerations dominate decision-making, the outcomes measured must reflect the full range of values and benefits sought. When the cost-effectiveness of family planning programmes was measured by births averted, the emphasis was on permanent methods (e.g., sterilization) over temporary (e.g., oral pills, IUDs, injectables and

Making health services better and more efficient requires a high initial investment.

5

barrier methods). Today, measures of cost-effectiveness seek to include the quality of care offered, including a range of contraceptives, and the advantage for the client of different methods at different stages of the life cycle.

Partnerships for Health

The consensus of governments and civil society alike is that ensuring access to health is primarily a public sector concern. At the same time, there is a discussion about the place of the private sector.

The ICPD Programme of Action recognizes that providing reproductive health services necessarily requires a partnership in which many institutions must participate. Assigning appropriate roles to different public and private sources, either as providers or as financiers of reproductive health services, is a matter for both principled debate and practical experimentation.[11]

Who Pays: How Should We Decide?

The World Bank estimates that less-developed countries not only spend less on health than higher-income countries, but often fund a smaller proportion of their health expenditure through public financing.

Recent studies of national health accounts in the Philippines[12] and Bangladesh[13] have confirmed that private

TABLE 2: Public and Private Health Expenditure[17]

	Health Expenditure		Health Expenditure per capita
	Public	Private	PPP
	% of GDP	% of GDP	$
World	2.5	2.7	527
Low income	1.0	3.2	52
Middle income	2.4	2.0	183
Lower middle income	2.2	1.7	119
Upper middle income	3.0	3.1	427
Low & middle income	1.8	2.5	133
East Asia & Pacific	1.8	1.8	118
Europe & Central Asia	3.9	1.0	279
Latin America & Caribbean	2.6	3.7	412
Middle East & N. Africa	2.3	2.4	176
South Asia	0.8	3.8	57
Sub-Saharan Africa	1.7	1.5	82
High income	6.0	3.6	2,280

Source: The World Bank 1999. *World Development Indicators 1999.* Washington D.C.: The World Bank.

out-of-pocket expenditures for reproductive health are larger than previously recognized and can exceed public expenditures. Much health expenditure, public or private, goes to curative care; if money is needed in a medical crisis, people do whatever they can to find it. Reproductive health care on the other hand is largely preventive so there is less willingness to pay for it, and family planning prevents not disease but pregnancy.

Reliance on private resources for reproductive health services varies considerably. In such countries as Brazil and Colombia, for example, non-governmental organizations play a major role in reproductive health service delivery. In other Latin American countries, state involvement is limited by cultural and political considerations, or the private sector is preferred. More than half of all health expenditures in Latin America may be financed from private allocations,[14] and the proportion of reproductive health care privately financed is probably even larger. In Africa and in many Asian countries, the state is a major provider of services.[15]

The arguments for government and official donor funding of reproductive health services, and other development strategies of the Programme of Action, are fundamental.[16] Governments and donors should subsidize:

- Services to which society believes each individual should have access regardless of their ability to pay;

- Activities to benefit not only the individual but society as a whole;

Increased reliance on the private sector must not deprive the poor of health services.

- Services the private sector has little or no incentive to provide;

- Services that help reduce poverty.

The first of these arguments is based on principles of equity and rights. The right to health, the right to non-discrimination with regard to gender, and the right to choose the number and spacing of one's children are basic parts of existing human rights.[18]

The second recognizes general benefits to society. These include, for example: reduced social impact of sexually transmitted diseases; lower public costs as the result of population growth and associated environmental degradation; and faster development as the result of the increased participation of women.

The third justifies investments in reproductive health service regulation and monitoring, testing, research and development. It also justifies support for information on reproductive health, which can help generate demand that can allow private-sector approaches to develop. However, the Programme of Action leaves it up to countries to decide the principles for allocating responsibilities to different actors. Similarly, the importance of a comprehensive set of integrated services is clearly stated but no blueprint is provided. This approach recognizes national priorities and provides a place for local inputs, capacities, perspectives, values and ingenuity.

The final argument recognizes the special susceptibility of the poor to ill-health and unwanted pregnancy, which makes it more difficult for poor people to escape poverty.

5

Making Sure Reproductive Health Services Reach the Poor

For many, the logical approach would be to ask those who can to pay, and to provide public services only to the poor. However, such a restriction risks undermining political support: if only the poor benefit from a programme, decision makers may reduce budgetary provision for it, particularly in the context of shrinking government budgets.[19]

It is difficult, moreover, to direct public inputs successfully. Political pressures bias services in favour of elite or urban populations, which accounts for the large share of health budgets going to city hospitals. Even without such pressures, the better-educated and better-off are better informed and more confident in dealing with public bureaucracies. Poor and marginalized people get little attention from public servants.

Public money can be saved if those who are able to pay do so, either through being shifted to private providers or by paying fees for public service. However, setting maximum income levels and administering means tests for service recipients is politically risky, time-consuming, and may cost more than it saves.

Evidence about service use by different population groups is clearer in family planning than in other areas of reproductive health care. Studies in Viet Nam, the Philippines and Indonesia show that the poorest fifth of the population receives about 15 per cent of the service benefits from public investment in family planning, and the poorest two fifths nearly 36 per cent — less in each case than their share of the population.

However, the poorest fifth get less than 9 per cent of national income, and the poorest two fifths get only 22 per cent; so that when compared to income distribution, family planning subsidies do transfer resources to the poor. Also, a large share of the health benefits going to higher income groups are accounted for by their disproportionate use of more costly hospital providers. Charging for these services would further help to direct public benefits to poorer people.

In Mexico, NGOs have had better success than the government programme in directing services to the poor because they can select their target population. The clients of FEMAP (Federación Mexicana de Asociaciones Privadas de Salud y Desarrollo Comunitario, AC), for example, include a higher proportion of poor people on the urban fringes than do government programmes.[20]

Drawing more revenue from those able to pay for use of higher-cost services, and working with NGOs and the private sector to reach selected populations, can improve the effectiveness of public services and provide the resources for improvements in quality — for example, for training staff to provide better service.

Many analysts have recommended increased reliance on the private sector for the most efficient delivery of reproductive health services. The challenge is to do this without depriving the many people in developing countries who cannot pay. A successful shift calls for more, not less, investment in reproductive health, to test different options for service delivery and finance and understand their impacts on quality and equity. It means more, not less, need for external resources to provide specialized technical assistance.

The donor community must accept its responsibility and remember their own systems of subsidized care and the development of their own public/private balance. Private initiatives are important but not at the expense of services for the poor. Faster development and improvements in health depend on greater access to services.

At the same time, communities are able and willing to share risks and costs to improve reproductive health services. One project in the Philippines has started a social insurance system to share the considerable costs of emergency obstetric care for the one pregnancy in 10 in which complications occur. An insurance scheme would cost $2.48 per insured pregnancy, but the expected economic benefit of the scheme would be nearly twice these costs.[21] Direct beneficiaries must still find part of the true costs, which remains a heavy burden on the poorest; but individuals and families are willing to do whatever is needed to find the money for life-saving care, and the scheme lowers the cost for all.

In Nepal, some communities have also pooled their resources to finance emergency transportation for obstetric care.[22] Combined with education for husbands in the risks, in the danger signs of complications and in support of prompt care, emergency referral can save many women's lives.

Community contributions may also take the form of repair, maintenance and general upkeep. Communities can often provide materials or construction to supplement public provision of staff and salaries.

Fees for service can help maintain programmes, but there is a question— do fees reduce access and discourage use of health services? The evidence is mixed: some studies have found that service use falls off when fees are first imposed, but may recover over time. Some studies show that fees are more acceptable when a part is directed towards improvements in service quality, and may be followed by increased service use.[23]

Conclusion

Despite tight resources and other constraints, both developed and developing countries have built new partnerships among governments and civil society for population and development, created integrated programmes for sexual and reproductive health, and advanced the empowerment of women. This progress shows that the ICPD goals are seen as necessary and practical.

In an age of globalization, providing basic social services is a global responsibility. The alternative to assistance for long-term investment in development, including population, is the increasing likelihood of social breakdown and an increasing demand for short-term relief. Addressing the effects of social breakdown will save lives, but addressing the causes will allow people, and nations, to build lives of their own.

5

Notes

Chapter 1

1. Murray, Christopher J. L., and Alan D. Lopez (eds.). 1996. *The Global Burden of Disease: A Comprehensive Assessment of Mortality and Disability from Diseases, Injuries and Risk Factors in 1990 and Projected to 2020.* Published by the Harvard School of Public Health on behalf of the World Health Organization and the World Bank. Cambridge, Massachusetts: Harvard University Press.

2. United Nations Development Programme. 1998. *Human Development Report 1998.* New York and London: Oxford University Press.

3. See, for example: Sanderson, Warren. 1994. "Simulation Models of Demographic, Economic, and Environmental Interactions." In *Population, Development, Environment: Understanding Their Interactions in Mauritius*, edited by Wolfgang Lutz, et al. Berlin: Springer-Verlag. Recent evidence suggests that sea level fluctuations associated with past cycles of Ice Ages took place only within decades and that the Antarctic climate is currently undergoing unexpectedly rapid change. See: Stevens, William K. 7 July 1998. "Catastrophic Melting of Ice Sheet is Possible, Studies Hint." *The New York Times*; and Stevens, William K. 16 February 1999. "In Ancient Ice Ages, Clues to Climate." *The New York Times.*

4. The Office of the United Nations High Commissioner for Refugees (UNHCR) estimates that some 50 million people around the world might legitimately be described as victims of forced displacement: around 22 million who are of direct concern to UNHCR (refugees, people who are stateless or whose nationality is disputed, and some internally displaced people), an additional 20 million internally displaced people for whom the organization has no responsibility, and around 3 million Palestinian refugees who are assisted by the United Nations Relief and Works Agency for Palestine Refugees in the Near East. Figures from UNHCR Web site: <www.unhcr.ch>.

5. The emerging consensus on the important role of demographic factors in economic development is summarized in the report of the Symposium on Population Change and Economic Development, 2-6 November 1999, held in Bellagio, Italy and sponsored by the Rockefeller and Packard Foundations. The dynamics were discussed at length in: UNFPA. 1998a. *The State of World Population 1998: The New Generations.* New York: UNFPA.

6. UNFPA. 1999a. *Southeast Asian Populations in Crisis: Challenges to the Implementation of the ICPD Programme of Action.* New York: UNFPA.

7. The effect of education of parents (and particularly of mothers) on fertility has long been established in demographic social research (A recent review can be found in: Bledsoe, Caroline, et al. 1999. *Critical Perspectives on Schooling and Fertility in the Developing World.* Committee on Population, Commission on Behavioral and Social Sciences and Education, National Research Council. Washington, D.C.: National Academy Press.). Results on the relation to children's schooling are reported in: Montgomery, Mark R., Mary Arends-Kuenning, and Cem Mete. 1999. *The Quantity-Quality Transition in Asia.* Policy and Research Division, Working Paper 123. New York: The Population Council.

8. See: Mroz, Thomas A., et al. 1999. "Quality, Accessibility, and Contraceptive Use in Rural Tanzania." *Demography* 36(1): 23-40.

9. Wall, L. 1998. "The Social Context of Maternal Morbidity and Mortality Among the Hausa of Northern Nigeria." *Studies in Family Planning* 29(4): 343. New York: The Population Council.

10. UNFPA. 1998b. *Report of the Round Table on Adolescent Sexual and Reproductive Rights: Key Future Actions.* New York: UNFPA.

11. Data on prevalence increases among injecting drug users and other high-risk behaviour populations are reported in: The World Bank. 1997. *Confronting AIDS: Public Priorities in a Global Epidemic*, chapter 2. New York: Oxford University Press. Simulations show that increases in prevalence in populations with unprotected commercial sex and casual sex practitioners develop more slowly but can still advance from negligible to over 15 per cent prevalence in the general population within ten years. Studies of social network influences on HIV/AIDS transmission demonstrate that a general pandemic can develop rapidly in populations with relatively few women with multiple partners and few high-risk groups when some infected men engage in relationships concurrently rather than sequentially, and that this may have been the case in the development of the general pandemic in Uganda (Morris, Martina. 1999. "Sexual Networks and HIV: The Population Dynamics of Infectious Disease." Presentation at the Population Council, New York, New York, 4 March 1999).

12. Women-headed households constitute a sizeable and growing proportion of the poor (United Nations. 1995. *The World's Women: Trends and Statistics*, Second Edition (Sales No. E95/XVI.2). Social Statistics and Indicators Series K, No. 12. New York: United Nations). Some exaggeration of the growth of women's relative deprivation may have entered the discourse (see: Marcoux, Alain. 1998. "The Feminization of Poverty: Claims, Facts, and Data Needs." *Population and Development Review* 24(1): 131-139. New York: The Population Council.). However, data on the poverty of rural women and of older women firmly identify increases in the proportions of the poor who are women.

13. UNFPA. 1999b. *Report of the 1998 UNFPA Field Inquiry: Progress in the Implementation of the ICPD Programme of Action.* New York: UNFPA.

14. UNFPA. 5 June 1998. "Winners of 1998 United Nations Population Award Announced." Press release. New York: UNFPA.

15. An overview of the principles, practice and impact of communication is found in: Piotrow, Phyllis, et al. 1997. *Health Communication: Lessons from Family Planning and Reproductive Health.* Westport, Connecticut: Praeger.

16. See further: The World Bank. 1998. *Assessing Aid.* New York: Oxford University Press.

Chapter 2

1. The statistics reported in this section represent shares of the 114 countries that responded to the UNFPA survey whose results are presented in: UNFPA. 1999. *Report of the 1998 UNFPA Field Inquiry: Progress in the Implementation of the ICPD Programme of Action.* New York: UNFPA.

2. Some of the longest established population policies and programmes are found in Asia. India, for example, which had a long tradition of censuses and record-taking, can date its concern with population issues back to the mid-1950s. Like other countries with long-established policies, it was necessary to update the policies, strategies and institutional frameworks to be consistent with the principles of the Programme of Action. Other countries with less established policy frameworks have created policies that reflect recent population and development concerns.

3. United Nations. 1998a. *World Population Prospects (The 1998 Revision).* New York: United Nations.

4. The demographic transition was first described by Frank Notestein (see: Notestein, Frank. 1953. "Economic Problems of Population Change." In *Proceedings of the Eighth International Conference of Agricultural Economists*, pp. 13-31. London: Oxford University Press.). He theorized that traditional agricultural societies needed high fertility to offset high mortality rates; that urbanization, industrialization, education, and the accompanying economic and social change caused a decline in deaths, particularly infant mortality rates; and that fertility then fell as children became more expensive and less valuable in economic terms.

5. Two of the best known such studies are: Coale, Ansley J., and Susan Cotts Watkins (eds.). 1986. *The Decline of Fertility in Europe.* Princeton, New Jersey: Princeton University Press; and Cleland, John, and Chris Wilson. 1987. "Demand Theories of the Fertility Decline: An Iconoclastic View." *Population Studies* 41(1): 5-30.

6. Bongaarts, John, and Susan Cotts Watkins. 1996. "Social Interactions and Contemporary Fertility Transitions." *Population and Development Review* 22(4): 639-682. New York: The Population Council.

7. Bulatao, Rodolfo A. 1998. *The Value of Family Planning Programs in Developing Countries.* Santa Monica, California: Rand Corporation.

8. Even those who note the role of women's education, increased communication and mobility and other aspects of social and economic development recognize the important role of national programmes. See, for example: Caldwell, John C., et al. 1999. "The Bangladesh Fertility Decline: An Interpretation." *Population and Development Review* 22(1): 67 84. New York: The Population Council.

9. Bongaarts, John. 1999. "The Role of Family Planning Programs in Contemporary Fertility Transitions." In *The Continuing Demographic Transition*, edited by G.W. Jones and J. Caldwell. London: Oxford University Press.

10. Bongaarts and Watkins 1996.

11. A scientific review of the concept of social diffusion and its relation to other explanations of demographic transition can be found in: Reed, Holly, Rona Briere, and John Casterline (eds.). 1999. *The Role of Diffusion Processes in Fertility Change in Developing Countries: Report of a Workshop.* Washington, D.C.: National Academy Press; and forthcoming publications of the papers of the January 1998 workshop sponsored by the Committee on Population of the National Academy of Science.

12. The Population Division prepares high, medium and low variant projections which theoretically encompass the plausible range of demographic outcomes through 2050. While the medium variant is often misrepresented as a prediction, it is simply the mathematical outcome of a group of assumptions about future fertility and mortality. Until recently these projections were not accurate more than a decade or so into the future, and the revisions sometimes result in significantly higher or lower long-term projections. Nonetheless, the projections serve a useful planning tool for both national and international population policy and social planning.

13. See: Lutz, Wolfgang, James W. Waupel, and Dennis A. Ahlburg (eds.). 1999. *Frontiers of Population Forecasting.* A Supplement to Volume 24. *Population and Development Review.* 1998. New York: The Population Council.

14. Literacy rates are usually derived from data on self-declared literacy on censuses or from updating census or survey estimates with current estimates of school enrolment, not criteria-based literacy tests. Although UNESCO has issued guidelines for estimating literacy levels, international comparability is affected by differences in methods and completeness of coverage. A full report of educational statistics, derived from the primary UNESCO and other supplementary data, can be found in: The World Bank. 1998. *World Development Indicators 1998.* Washington, D.C.: The World Bank.

15. Net primary enrolment measures the percentage of the school-age population that is enroled in primary education. Data are typically collected at the beginning of each school year; a more accurate measure of participation rates would require data on daily attendance by age, grade, and gender. Secondary enrolment figures are likely to be biased upwards, because data are often based on assumptions about promotion, repetition and attrition rather than actual student records. (The World Bank 1998, p. 37.)

16. Some sub-regions also experienced enrolment declines at some grade levels in the 1980s, but did not regress to 1960 levels. See: United Nations Educational, Social and Cultural Organization. 1998. *Trends and Projections of Enrolment by Level of Education, by Age, and by Sex 1960-2030 (as Assessed in 1998)*. Paris: United Nations Educational, Social and Cultural Organization.

17. The Population Council. 1996. *The Unfinished Transition*. The Population Council Issues Papers. New York: The Population Council.

18. See: Filmer, Deon, and Lant Pritchett. 1999. "The Effect of Household Wealth on Educational Attainment: Evidence from 35 Countries." *Population and Development Review* 25(1): 85-120. New York: The Population Council.

19. See: Filmer and Pritchett 1999; and Knodel, Johan, and Gavin Jones. 1996. "Post-Cairo Population Policy: Does Promoting Girls' Schooling Miss the Mark?" *Population and Development Review* 22(4): 683-702, 814, 816. New York: The Population Council.

20. For a complete analysis of the statistics and challenges of adult literacy and education, see: United Nations Educational, Social and Cultural Organization. 1997a. *Adult Education in a Polarizing World*. Paris: United Nations Educational, Social and Cultural Organization.

21. This relationship is regularly graphed in the *World Eduction Report* series. See, for example: United Nations Educational, Social and Cultural Organization. 1997b. *World Education Report 1997*. Paris: United Nations Educational, Social and Cultural Organization. See also: Cleland, J., and J. van Ginneken. 1988. "Maternal Education and Child Survival in Developing Countries: The Search for Pathways of Influence." *Social Science and Medicine* 27: 1357-1368. An important early theoretical discussion of the relationships can be found in: Cochrane, Susan H. 1979. *Fertility and Education: What Do We Really Know?* Baltimore, Maryland: The Johns Hopkins University Press.

22. See: Diamond, Ian, Margaret Newby, and Sarah Varle. "Female Education and Fertility: Examining the Links." In *Critical Perspectives on Schooling and Fertility in the Developing World*, edited by Caroline H. Bledsoe, et al. 1999. Committee on Population, Commission on Behavioral and Social Sciences and Education, National Research Council. Washington, D.C.: National Academy Press.

23. See: Cleland, J., and G. Kaufman. 1993. "Education, Fertility, and Child Survival: Unravelling the Links." Paper prepared for the International Union for the Scientific Study of Population Committee on Anthropology and Demography Seminar, Barcelona, Spain, 10-14 November. Liége, Belgium: International Union for the Scientific Study of Population.

24. See, for example: Cochrane, Susan H., M. A. Khan, and Ibrahim K. T. Osheba. 1990. "Education, Income, and Desired Fertility in Egypt: A Revised Perspective." *Economic Development and Cultural Change* 38(2): 313-339.

25. Bledsoe, Caroline H., Jennifer A. Johnson-Kuhn, and John G. Haaga. "Introduction." In Bledsoe, et al. 1999.

26. A detailed examination of the implications of population ageing was reported in: UNFPA. 1998. *The State of World Population 1998: The New Generations*. New York: UNFPA.

27. Ibid.

28. World Health Organization. 1999. *The World Health Report 1999: Making a Difference*. Geneva: World Health Organization.

29. For a good synthesis and overview of demography, reproductive health and AIDS, see: Goliber, Thomas J. 1997. *Population and Reproductive Health in Sub-Saharan Africa: Population Bulletin* 52, No. 4. Washington, D.C.: Population Reference Bureau.

30. UNFPA. (Forthcoming.) *AIDS Update 1998*. New York: UNFPA.

31. Bongaarts, John, and Griffith Feeney. 1998. *On the Quantum and Tempo of Fertility*. Policy Research Division Working Papers No. 109. New York: The Population Council.

32. Frejka, Thomas, and John Ross. (Forthcoming.) "The Course to Below Replacement Fertility: A Review of the Empirical Evidence." Special Supplement to *Population and Development Review* on the Demographic Transition. New York: The Population Council.

33. Such floors have been noted in some Latin American countries and in Bangladesh (Caldwell, et al. 1999.).

34. For a complete set of global, regional and national urbanization statistics, see: United Nations. 1998b. *World Urbanization Prospects: The 1996 Revision*. New York: Population Division, Department of Economic and Social Affairs, United Nations. The updated 1998 revision is in preparation.

35. Urbanization trends and implications were the subject of: UNFPA. 1996. *The State of World Population 1996: Changing Places: Population,*

Development and the Urban Future. New York: UNFPA.

36. Ibid.

37. United Nations. 1996. *Trends in Total Migrant Stock.* Revision 4 (POP/1B/DB/96/1/Rev.4). Database. New York: Population Division, Department of Economic and Social Affairs, United Nations.

38. Zlotnick, Hania. 1998. "International Migration Levels, Trends and What Existing Data Systems Reveal." In *Technical Symposium on International Migration and Development.* United Nations Task Force on Basic Social Services for All (BSSA), vol. 1, The Hague, Netherlands, 29 June-3 July 1998.

39. Ibid.

40. Ibid.

41. Malthus, Thomas R. 1798. *An Essay on the Principle of Population.* London: Printed for J. Johnson, in St. Paul's Church-Yard.

42. Meadows, Donella, et al. 1972. *The Limits to Growth: A Report for the Club of Rome's Project on the Predicament of Mankind.* New York: Universe; and Ehrlich, Paul R. 1968. *The Population Bomb.* New York: Ballantine.

43. See: "Estimates of Human Carrying Capacity: A Survey of Four Centuries." In *How Many People Can the Earth Support?* by Joel E. Cohen. 1995. New York: Norton & Company.

44. See: Brown, Lester R., Gary Gardner, and Brian Halweil. 1999. *Beyond Malthus: Nineteen Dimensions of the Population Challenge.* Washington: WorldWatch Institute.

45. United States Department of Agriculture (USDA). 1998. *Production, Supply and Distribution (PS&D)* (electronic database). Washington, D.C.: United States Department of Agriculture. See also: Brown, Gardner and Halweil 1999.

46. See Reid, T.R. 1998. "Feeding the Planet." *National Geographic,* No. 4 (October 1998): 56-75.

47. Seckler, David, David Molden, and Randolph Barker. 1999. "Water Scarcity in the Twenty-first Century." *International Journal of Water Resources Development* 15(1&2): 29-43. See also: Brown, Gardner and Halweil 1999.

48. de Onis, M., et al. 1998. "The Worldwide Magniture of Protein-Energy Malnutrition: An Overview from the WHO Global Database on Child Growth." Geneva: World Health Organization. See also: Brown, Gardner and Halweil. 1999.

49. United States Department of Agriculture (USDA). 1998; United States Department of Agriculture (USDA). 1991. "World Grain Database." Unpublished printout, Washington, D.C.: United States Department of Agriculture (USDA); and United States Bureau of the Census. 1998. *International Data Base* (electronic database), updated 30 November 1998. Washington, D.C.: United States Bureau of the Census.

50. Intergovernmental Panel on Climate Change. 1990. *Climate Change: The IPCC Scientific Assessment.* Cambridge, United Kingdom: Cambridge University Press; and Intergovernmental Panel on Climate Change. 1995. *IPCC Working Group I Summary for Policymakers.* Cambridge, United Kingdom: Cambridge University Press.

Chapter 3

1. World Health Organization and United Nations Children's Fund. 1996. *Revised 1990 Estimates of Maternal Mortality* (WHO/FRH/MSM/96.11 and UNICEF/PLN/96.1). Geneva: World Health Organization and New York: United Nations Children's Fund.

2. World Health Organization. 1998a. "Global and Regional Estimates of Incidence of Mortality Due to Unsafe Abortion with a Listing of Available Country Data" (WHO/RHT/MSM/97.16). Geneva: World Health Organization.

3. This chapter is based primarily on a 1998 UNFPA field enquiry with responses from 114 countries and on country case studies conducted in 22 countries in Asia (Bangladesh, Pakistan, Nepal, India, Sri Lanka, Indonesia and the Philippines), Africa (Burkina Faso, Côte d'Ivoire, Ghana, Senegal, South Africa, Tanzania, Uganda and Zambia), the Near East (Jordan, Egypt, and Morocco) and Latin America and the Caribbean (Brazil, Jamaica, Mexico and Peru) by UNFPA, the Futures Group Policy Project, the Population Reference Bureau, Family Care International and the Center for International Cooperation, New York University. Hardee, K., et al. 1998. *Post-Cairo Reproductive Health Policies and Programs: A Comparative Study of Eight Countries.* Policy Occasional Working Paper 2. Washington, D.C.: The Futures Group International; Ashford, L., and C. Makinson. 1999. *Reproductive Health in Policy and Practice.* Washington, DC: Population Reference Bureau; Family Care International. 1998a. *Implementation of ICPD Commitments on Women's Reproductive and Sexual Health: A Report of Four African Countries.* New York: Family Care International; Family Care International. 1998b. *Implementation of ICPD Commitments on Women's Reproductive and Sexual Health: A South Asia Report.* New York: Family Care International; and Forman, S., and R. Ghosh. 1999. *Paying for Essentials: The Reproductive Health Approach to Population and Development.* Policy Paper Series. New York: Center on International Cooperation, New York University.

4. UNFPA. 1998a. *Ensuring Reproductive Rights and Implementing Sexual and Reproductive Health Programmes Including Women's Empowerment, Male Involvement and Human Rights.* Report of the Expert Round Table Meeting, Kampala, Uganda,

22-25 June 1998. New York: UNFPA; and UNFPA. 1999a. *Report of the International Forum for the Operational Review and Appraisal of the Implementation of the Programme of Action of the International Conference on Population and Development*, The Hague, Netherlands, 8-12 February 1999. New York: UNFPA. These reports are available on UNFPA's Web site: <www.unfpa.org>.

5. Weighted by the number of married women of reproductive age. This estimation was made for 1990-1995. United Nations. 1998a. *World Population Monitoring 1996. Selected Aspects of Reproductive Rights and Reproductive Health*. New York: Population Division, Department of Economic and Social Affairs, United Nations.

6. Barnett, B., and J. Stein. 1998. *Women's Voices, Women's Lives: The Impact of Family Planning*. Research Triangle Park, North Carolina: Family Health International.

7. UNFPA. 1998b. *Donor Support for Contraceptive Commodities 1996*. New York: UNFPA.

8. Includes UNICEF, UNFPA, the World Bank, WHO, IPPF and the Population Council.

9. Starrs, A. 1998. *The Safe Motherhood Action Agenda: Priorities for the Next Decade*. Report on the Safe Motherhood Technical Meeting, Colombo, Sri Lanka, 18-23 October, 1997. New York: Family Care International; and Maine, D., and A. Rosenfield. 1999. "The Safe Motherhood Initiative: Why Has It Stalled?" *American Journal of Public Health* (89)4: 480-482.

10. Pathak, Laxmi Raj, et al. 1998. *Maternal Mortality and Morbidity Study*. Kathmandu, Nepal: Family Health Division, Department of Health Services, Ministry of Health, His Majesty's Government of Nepal.

11. United Nations. 1999a. *World Abortion Policies 1999* (Sales No. E.99.XIII.5). New York. United Nations.

12. Rahman, A., L. Katzive, and S.K. Henshaw. 1998. "A Global Review of Laws on Induced Abortion." *International Family Planning Perspectives* 24(2): 56-64. The study looked at 152 nations and independent territories with a population of 1 million or more.

13. Westoff, C.W., et al. 1998. *Replacement of Abortion by Contraception in Three Central Asian Republics: Final Study Report*. Calverton, Maryland: Macro International Inc. and Washington, D.C.: Policy Project.

14. Ardayfio, Rosemary. 1999. "Midwives to the Rescue." *People and the Planet*. 8(1). Web site: <www.oneworld.org/patp/>.

15. Family Care International 1998b.

16. Joint United Nations Programme on HIV/AIDS (UNAIDS). 1997. *Impact of HIV and Sexual Health Education on the Sexual Behaviour of Young People: A Review Update* (UNAIDS/97.4). A Best Practice Collection. Geneva: Joint United Nations Programme on HIV/AIDS.

17. Shongwe, T. 1998. "The Swaziland Schools HIV/AIDS and Population Education (SPAPE) Programme." In *Confounding the Critics: Cairo, Five Years On: Conference Report: Cocoyoc, Morelos, Mexico, 15-18 November 1998*, by HERA: Health, Empowerment, Rights and Accountability. 1998. New York: International Women's Health Coalition.

18. UNFPA. 1999. *A Five-Year Review of Progress towards the Implementation of the Programme of Action of the International Conference on Population and Development*. Background paper prepared for The Hague Forum, The Hague, Netherlands, 8-12 February 1999. New York: UNFPA; and UNFPA. 1998c. *AIDS Update 1998*. New York: UNFPA.

19. United Nations. 1994. *Report of the International Conference on Population and Development (Cairo, 5-13 September 1994)* (A/Conf. 171/13), paragraph 4.22. New York: United Nations.

20. Center for Reproductive Law and Policy. 1999. *Female Circumcision/Female Genital Mutilation: Global Laws and Policies Towards Elimination*. New York: Center for Reproductive Law and Policy. Web site: <www.clrp.org>.

21. Sadasivam, B. 1999. *Risks, Rights and Reforms: A 50-Country Survey Assessing Government Actions Five Years after the International Conference on Population and Development*. New York: Women's Environment and Development Organization.

22. UNFPA. 1997a. *United Nations Population Fund: Proposed Projects and Programmes: Recommendation by the Executive Director: Assistance to the Government of China* (DP/FPA/CP/196). Third Regular Session 1997 of the Executive Board of the United Nations Development Programme and of the United Nations Population Fund. New York: UNFPA.

23. UNFPA. 1997b. *The State of the World Population 1997. The Right to Choose: Reproductive Rights and Reproductive Health*. New York: UNFPA.

24. Merrick, T. (Forthcoming.) "Delivering Reproductive Health Services in Health Reform Settings: Challenges and Opportunities." Washington, D.C.: The World Bank. Web site: <www.worldbank.org>.

25. Sadasivam 1999.

26. Askew, I., G. Fassihian, and N. Maggwa. 1998. "Integrating STI and HIV/AIDS Services at MCH/Family Planning Clinics." In *Clinic-Based Family Planning and Reproductive Health Services in Africa: Findings from Situation Analysis Studies*, edited by K. Miller, et al. 1998. New York: The Population Council.

27. Family Care International. 1998c. *Implementation of ICPD Commitments on Women's Reproductive*

and Sexual Health: Zambia Country Report. New York: Family Care International.

28. Family Care International. 1998d. *Implementation of ICPD Commitments on Women's Reproductive and Sexual Health: Sri Lanka Country Report.* New York: Family Care International.

29. Source: Hardee, et al. 1998.

30. Bruce, J. 1990. "Fundamental Elements of Quality of Care: A Simple Framework." *Studies in Family Planning* 21(2): 61-91.

31. Kols, A.J., and J.E. Sherman. 1998. *Family Planning Programs: Improving Quality.* Population Reports. Series J. No. 47. Baltimore, Maryland: Population Information Program, Johns Hopkins University.

32. McFarlane, C., et al. 1996. "The Quality of Jamaica Public Sector and NGO Family Planning Services: Perspectives of Providers and Clients." Final Study Report; Ndhlovu, l. 1995. *Quality of Care in Family Planning Service Delivery in Kenya: Clients' and Providers' Perspectives.* Final Report. Nairobi: Ministry of Health and Population Council; and Tavrow, P., D. Namate, and N. Mpemba. 1995. "Quality of Care: An Assessment of Family Planning Providers Attitudes and Client-Provider Interactions in Malawi." Unpublished paper.

33. Ashford and Makinson 1999.

34. Gorishti, E., and J. Haffey. ND. "'We Want to Know Everything About It': Albanian Women Speak About Family Planning." Arlington, Virginia: John Snow, Inc. SEATS II.

35. Barnett and Stein 1998.

36. Mroz, T.A., et al. 1999. "Quality, Accessibility and Contraceptive Use in Rural Tanzania." *Demography* 36(1): 23-40.

37. Schuler, S., and Z. Hossain. 1998. "Family Planning Clinics Through Women's Eyes and Voices: A Case Study from Rural Bangladesh." *International Family Planning Perspectives* 24(4): 171.

38. Haberland, N., et al. 1998. "Unutilized Capacity and Missed Opportunities in Family Planning Services." In Miller et al. 1998.

39. Sathar, Z.A., and J.B. Casterline. 1998. "The Onset of Fertility Transition in Pakistan." *Population and Development Review* 24(4): 773-796. New York: The Population Council.

40. Haberland et al. 1998.

41. Kols and Sherman 1998.

42. Ibid.

43. Lynam, P.F., L.M. Rabinowitz, and M. Shobowale. 1993. "Using Self-Assessment to Improve the Quality of Family Planning Clinic Services." *Studies in Family Planning* 24(4): 252-260.

44. Murphy, E.M., and C. Steele. 1997. "Client-Provider Interactions (CPI) In Family Planning Services." In *Recommendations for Updating Selected Practices in Contraceptive Use*, vol. 1, by Technical Guidelines / Competence Working Group, USAID. 1997. Chapel Hill, North Carolina: INTRAH.

45. El Gebaly, H., et al. 1998. "Egypt's Gold Star Program: Improving Care and Raising Expectations." In Kols and Sherman 1998, pp. 20-21.

46. McCauley, A.P., and C. Salter. 1995. "Meeting the Needs of Young Adults." *Population Reports.* Series J. No. 41. Baltimore, Maryland: Population Information Program, Johns Hopkins University.

47. An excellent source book of practical advice and case examples concerning health communications in the area of reproductive health is: Piotrow, Phyllis Tilson, et al. 1997. *Health Communication: Lessons from Family Planning and Reproductive Health.* Westport, Connecticut: Praeger Press (published under the auspices of the Center for Communications Programs, Johns Hopkins School of Public Health).

48. Buffington, S. deCastro. 1995. "A Framework for Establishing Integrated Reproductive Health Training." *Advances in Contraception* 11: 317-324.

49. Kols and Sherman 1998.

50. Bianco, M. 1998. "Monitoring Implementation of the Cairo Programme of Action As A Women's Citizenship Practice in Five Latin American Countries." In *Confounding the Critics: Cairo, Five Years On: Conference Report: Cocoyoc, Morelos, Mexico, 15-18 November 1998*, by HERA: Health, Empowerment, Rights and Accountability. 1998. New York: International Women's Health Coalition.

51. Joint United Nations Programme on HIV/AIDS (UNAIDS) 1997.

52. Barnett, B. 1997. "Gender Norms Affect Adolescents." *Network* 17(3): 10-13.

53. Mensch, B.S., J. Bruce, and M.E. Greene. 1998. *The Uncharted Passage: Girls' Adolescence in the Developing World.* New York: The Population Council.

54. Ngwana, A., and A. Akwi-Ogojo. 1996. *Adolescent Reproductive Health Rights in Sub-Saharan Africa.* Washington, D.C.: Center for Development and Population Activities (CEDPA).

55. Source: Barnett and Stein 1998.

56. Barnett, B. 1997. "Education Protects Health, Delays Sex." *Network* 17(3): 14-15, 18-20.

57. Gorishti, E., and J. Haffey. ND. "'We Want to Know Everything About It.' Romanian Women Speak About Family Planning." Arlington, Virginia: John Snow Inc. SEATS II.

58. McCauley and Salter 1995.

59. Hughes, J., and A.P. McCauley. 1998. "Improving the Fit: Adolescents' Needs and Future Programmes for Sexual and Reproductive Health in Developing Countries." *Studies in Family Planning* 29(2). 238-239.

60. Barnett and Stein 1998; and Schuler and Hossain 1998.

61. Barnett and Stein 1998.

62. For example, in the Central Asian republics in 1998, UNFPA and the Economic Cooperation Organization organized a conference on male involvement. Participating countries developed an action programme for increasing the role of men in reproductive health programmes. UNFPA. (Forthcoming.). ECO/UNFPA Conference on the Role of Men in Population and Reproductive health Programmes, Baku, Azerbaijan, 21-24 September 1998.

63. Ndong, I., et al. 1998. "Men's Reproductive Health: Defining, Designing and Delivering Services." *International Family Planning Perspectives* 25 (Supplement): S53-S55.

64. Office of the United Nations High Commissioner for Refugees. 1998. *Refugees and Others of Concern to UNHCR: 1997 Statistical Overview.* Geneva: Office of the United Nations High Commissioner for Refugees.

65. Partner NGOs include CARE International, the International Rescue Committee, John Snow Inc., Marie Stopes International and the Women's Commission for Refugee Women and Children.

66. UNFPA. 8 April 1998. "Emergency Reproductive Health Kits en Route to Kosovo Refugees." Press release. New York: UNFPA; and UNFPA. 9 April 1998. "Lives of Mothers and Newborns at Risk in Kosovo Crisis." New York: UNFPA.

67. UNFPA. 25 May 1999. "UNFPA Report Finds Incidences of Rape and Abduction Among Kosovo Refugees: Women Want to Speak Out." New York: UNFPA.

68. See: Office of the United Nations High Commissioner for Refugees' Web site <www.unhcr.ch>.

Chapter 4

1. UNFPA. 1998. *Civil Society and Population and Development.* Background document for the Round-table on Partnership with Civil Society in Implementation of the ICPD Programme of Action, Dhaka, Bangladesh, 27-30 July 1998.

2. NGOs in one narrow sense refer to those organizations accredited by the State to enter into contracts and other formal associations with donors and/or State bodies. Organizations whose operations and management overlap with the State and which operate as agents of the State, such as parastatal enterprises, are often excluded from the common understanding of NGOs.

3. UNFPA. 1999a. *Partnership with Civil Society to Implement the Programme of Action of the International Conference on Population and Development.* New York: Technical and Policy Division, UNFPA.

4. The reports of these forums, which were not a formal intergovernmental process, can be accessed through the ICPD+5 section of UNFPA's Web site (www.unfpa.org).

5. The international Micro-Credit Summit (Washington, D.C., 2-4 February 1997. Web site: <microcreditsummit.org>.) and the inclusion of micro-credit under the social protection programme of the World Bank are examples of the growing acceptance of this mechanism.

6. An interesting debate contrasts the approaches adopted under the Navrongo Community Health and Family Planning project in northern Ghana and the Consorcio Ramos Mujer in Peru. The former has been criticized by some (see, for example: Schuler, Sidney Ruth. 1999. "Gender and Community Participation in Reproductive Health Projects: Contrasting Models from Peru and Ghana." Paper presented at the Population Association of America Annual Meeting, New York, 25-27 March 1999.) for being based on a demographic rationale focussed on individual women's choices within a patriarchal setting; these critics applaud the women's association-based approach of the latter. However, it is interesting that despite their differing initial premises and rationales, the two programmes have started to converge as they develop. The Ghanaian project has facilitated the expansion of women's political role and representation in local conclaves and increasingly addressed the social context of women's decisions; the Peruvian women's groups have given greater attention to debates about whether and how to engage men in their action programmes. The basic wisdom of ICPD in recognizing the inseparability of empowerment in reproductive matters and other life spheres is ratified by the lessons learned while implementing these different approaches.

7. Sawalha, L. 1999. "Barriers of Silence: Reproductive Rights for Women in Jordan." *Development: Reproductive Health and Rights: Putting Cairo Into Action* 42(1): 41-46. Rome: Society for International Development.

8. Development Alternatives with Women for a New Era (DAWN). 1999. "Development Alternatives with Women for a New Era: Measuring Up Cairo." Christ Church, Barbados: Development Alternatives with Women for a New Era.

9. Pitanguy, J. 1999. "Reproductive Rights are Human Rights." *Development: Reproductive Health and Rights: Putting Cairo Into Action* 42(1): 11-14. Rome: Society for International Development.

10. UNFPA. 1999b. *Report of the 1998 UNFPA Field Inquiry.* New York: UNFPA.

11. Visaria, Leela, Shireen Jejeebhoy, and Tom Merrick. 1997. *From Family Planning to Reproductive Health: Challenges Facing India.* Paper presented in Session F.07 on Reproductive Health: Policy Development and Programme Implications, International Union for the Scientific Study of Population XXIII, General Population Conference, Beijing, China, 11-17 October 1997.

12. Family Care International. 1998. *Implementation of ICPD Commitments on Women's Reproductive and Sexual Health: Pakistan Country Report.* New York: Family Care International.

13. UNFPA. 1999c. *In Common Cause: Summary Report: Non-Governmental Organization Advisory Committee to UNFPA Recommendations and UNFPA Policies and Programmes: 1995, 1996, 1997.* Report.

14. Ibid.

15. Ibid.

16. "Honour killings" is a term used to describe the murder, at times by family members, of women suspected of or involved in sexual activity outside of traditionally proscribed bounds. It can include the murder of women already victims of sexual violence. Social ostracism is a less extreme, but often severe, manifestation of this blaming of the victims. Such practices are also used to restrict and control women's willing choices, even in the choice of life partners.

17. Family Care International 1998.

18. UNFPA 1999c.

19. Ibid.

20. Development Alternatives with Women for a New Era (DAWN) 1999.

21. Regional Meeting of NGOs from Latin America and the Spanish-Speaking Caribbean. 1998. *ICPD+5 Regional Assessment by NGOs from Latin America and the Spanish-Speaking Caribbean.* Report prepared for the ICPD+5 NGO Forum, The Hague, Netherlands, 5-6 February 1999.

22. UNFPA 1999c.

23. Ibid.

24. Ibid.

25. Bissell, S. 1999. "Grupo de Información en Reproducción Elegida (GIRE): Finding the Middle Ground for Women's Reproductive Rights." *Development: Reproductive Health and Rights: Putting Cairo Into Action* 42(1): 89-90. Rome: Society for International Development.

26. Bianco, M. 1998. "Monitoring Implementation of the Cairo Programme of Action As A Women's Citizenship Practice in Five Latin American Countries." In *Confounding the Critics: Cairo, Five Years On: Conference Report: Cocoyoc, Morelos, Mexico, 15-18 November 1998,* by HERA: Health, Empowerment, Rights and Accountability. 1998. New York: International Women's Health Coalition.

27. Sadasivam, B. 1999. *Risks, Rights and Reforms: A 50-Country Survey Assessing Government Actions Five Years After the International Conference on Population and Development.* New York: Women's Environment and Development Organization (WEDO).

28. Ibid.

29. UNFPA. 1999d. *Partnership with Civil Society. A Review of Progress since the International Conference on Population and Development.* A Report Prepared by the United Nations Population Fund for the NGO Forum on ICPD + 5, The Hague, Netherlands, 6-7 February, 1999. Technical Report No. 46. New York: UNFPA

30. Bissell, S., M.C. Mejia, and P. Mercado. 1998. "The National Forum of Women and Population Policy (Foro Nacional de Mujeres y Políticas de Población): NGO/Government Partnership for Reproductive Health in Mexico." In HERA: Health, Empowerment, Rights and Accountability 1998.

31. Abdullah, R. 1998. "Southeast Asia: Developing an Enabling Policy Environment for Building NGO-Government Relationships." In HERA: Health, Empowerment, Rights and Accountability 1998.

32. Canadian International Development Agency. 1999. *CIDA's Policy on Gender Equality.* Hull, Quebec: Canadian International Development Agency.

33. Organization for Economic Cooperation and Development. 1999. *Reaching the Goals in the S-21: Gender Equality and Health* (DCD/DAC/WID[99]2), vol. 2. Paris: Organization for Economic Cooperation and Development.

34. UNFPA 1999c.

35. See the report: Centre for Development and Population Activities. 1998. *Grassroots to Global Networks: Improving Women's Reproductive Health: ACCESS: Lessons Learned Conference.* Report of a meeting, 18-19 June 1998. Washington D.C.: Centre for Development and Population Activities.

36. Xaba, M., et al. 1998. "Transformation of Reproductive Health Services Project: South Africa: A Collaboration Between the Women's Health Project and Three Provincial Departments of Health and Welfare." In HERA: Health, Empowerment, Rights and Accountability 1998.

37. International Planned Parenthood Federation. 1999. *IPPF and Cairo+5 Bulletin,* Issue 8. London: International Planned Parenthood Federation.

38. NGO Forum and Youth Fora ICPD+5. *Report of The Hague, Netherlands: 6-7 February 1999.* Hilversum, Netherlands: World Population Foundation.

39. Organization for Economic Cooperation and Development 1999.

40. HealthWatch. 1998. "From Contraceptive Targets to Reproductive Health: India's Family Planning Programme after Cairo." In HERA: Health, Empowerment, Rights and Accountability 1998.

41. UNFPA 1999c.

42. Ibid.

43. These statistics are reported in: UNFPA 1999d.

44. UNFPA 1999c.

45. Alcala, M.J., Division for Latin America and the Caribbean, UNFPA. 1999. Personal Communication.

Chapter 5

1. *The 20/20 Initiative: Achieving Universal Access to Basic Social Services for Sustainable Human Development.* December 1994. Note prepared jointly by UNDP, UNESCO, UNFPA, UNICEF and WHO. New York: United Nations. This included $10-12 billion above the amount available for family planning in around 1990.

2. The evidence is extensively documented in a growing literature over the last decade. It is also clear from the importance given now in the international financial institutions to social protection and to efforts for debt relief. "Development with a human face" is changing from a slogan to a set of practical and pragmatic negotiations and instrumentalities.

3. Estimates of expenditure per capita were calculated by subregion and then expanded to encompass the regions' entire populations. Data are available from 89 developing countries, 18 donor countries, 5 international lending institutions, 11 foundations, 12 United Nations agencies or organizations, 77 national NGOs and 21 university/research institutions. The compiled and analyzed data will be reported in: UNFPA. (Forthcoming.) *Global Population Assistance Report 1998.* New York: UNFPA.

4. To advance this process, a meeting was held in Hanoi in October 1998 attended by 29 developing countries, 19 donor countries, 11 international NGOs and 13 multilateral development organizations. The participants adopted the "Hanoi Consensus on the 20/20 Initiative: Universal Access to Basic Social Services" and agreed that the current economic and financial crisis underscores the relevance of the 20/20 Initiative to protect access to basic social services for the most vulnerable people.

5. UNFPA. 1999. *Global Population Assistance Report 1997.* New York: UNFPA.

6. Estimates on public resources allocated to reproductive health are based on questionnaires sent to government ministries. A few case studies (cited in: Janowitz, Barbara, Diana Measham, and Caroline West. 1999. *Issues in the Financing of Family Planning Services in Sub-Saharan Africa.* Research Triangle, North Carolina: Family Health International.) indicate that this can understate totals derived from field observations and interviews.

7. A comprehensive review of the difficulties encountered in their work is provided in: Dekker, Ari. 1999. "Background Note on Measuring Resource Flows for Population Activities: Issues and Trends." Internal project document. The Hague: Netherlands Interdisciplinary Demographic Institute.

8. Information on fees charged for family planning and immunization, for example, are assessed in the Demographic and Health Surveys sponsored by USAID. However, there are practical limits on the number of additional questions which can be asked in an already complex inquiry and information on the source of services is subject to some misreporting.

9. Joint United Nations Programme on HIV/AIDS (UNAIDS) and Harvard School of Public Health. 1999. *Level and Flow of National and International Resources for the Response to HIV/AIDS: 1996-1997* (UNAIDS/99.25E). Geneva: Joint United Nations Programme on HIV/AIDS.

10. Many analysts, including McGreevey, et al. (McGreevey, William, et al. 1999. *Value for Money in Reproductive Health: Issues and Options for Governments and Donors.* Washington, D.C.: Planning and Finance Group, The Futures Group International.) have emphasized the unrealistic level of the costs resulting from a strategy focused on anti-retroviral medications, particularly in poor countries. Additional resources will be required for AIDS prevention efforts not included in the costed package of the ICPD, including specialized information and education programmes directed to high-risk populations, particularly where the pandemic is not yet generalized in the population.

11. A recent thoughtful and challenging presentation of the issues can be found in: Behrman, Jere R., and James C. Knowles. 1998. "Population and Reproductive Health: An Economic Framework for Policy Evaluation." *Population and Development Review* 24(4): 697-738. New York: The Population Council.

12. Herrin, Alejandro N., et al. 1996. "National Family Planning Expenditures of the Philippines: Estimates for 1994." Unpublished manuscript.

13. Allison, Christopher. 1998. Personal communication.

14. Calculations based on data in: Conly, Shanti. 1998. *Paying Their Fair Share.* Washington, D.C: Population Action International. Cited in Janowitz, Measham, and West 1999.

15. Private sector involvement has also been examined in: Bulatao, Rodolfo. 1998. *The Value of Family*

Planning Programs in Developing Countries. Santa Monica, California: Rand Corporation. The UNFPA Global Initiative on Reproductive Health Commodity Management (described in this report) has conducted meetings on the topic and will produce future papers. A theoretical framework for examination of financing decision in reproductive health is given in: Behrman and Knowles 1998.

16. This presentation relies heavily on: Janowitz, Measham and West 1999. See also: Behrman and Knowles 1998; McGreevey, et al. 1999; and Merrick, T. (Forthcoming.) "Delivering Reproductive Health Services in Health Reform Settings: Challenges and Opportunities." Washington, D.C.: The World Bank. Web site: <www.worldbank.org>.

17. Data are most recently available from 1990-1997.

18. For a more extended discussion, see: UNFPA. 1997. *State of World Population 1997: The Right to Choose: Reproductive Rights and Reproductive Health.* New York: UNFPA.

19. This point is made in a challenging review of primary health care strategies (Filmer, Deon, Jeffrey Hammer, and Lant Pritchett. 1998. "Health Policy in Poor Countries: Weak Links in the Chain." Policy Research Working Paper No. 1874. Washington, D.C.: The World Bank Development Research Group.).

20. See the work of Julia Walsh, Malcolm Potts and their colleagues in the Bay Area International Health Group (e.g., Sylvie, Marceau, Julia Walsh, Elizabeth Townes and Tim Wade. "Can Consumers in Developing Countries Afford Contraceptives?" Draft paper).

21. Details of the economic analysis are presented in: Behrman and Knowles 1998.

22. For details see: Pathak, Laxmi Raj, et al. 1998. *Maternal Mortality and Morbidity Study.* Kathmandu, Nepal: Family Health Division, Department of Health Services, Ministry of Health, His Majesty's Government of Nepal.

23. See: Janowitz, Measham, and West 1999; Berman and Knowles 1998; and McGreevey, et al. 1999.

	Indicators of Mortality			Indicators of Education	
	Infant mortality Total per 1,000 live births	Life expectancy M / F	Maternal mortality ratio	Primary enrolment (gross) M / F	Proportion reaching grade 5 M / F
World Total	57	63.3 / 67.6			
More-developed regions (*)	9	71.1 / 78.7			
Less-developed regions (+)	63	61.8 / 65.0			
Least-developed countries (‡)	99	49.6 / 51.5			
Africa (1)	87	50.0 / 52.8			
Eastern Africa	101	44.4 / 46.4			
Burundi	119	41.0 / 43.8	1,300	55 / 46	76 / 78
Eritrea	91	49.3 / 52.4	1,400	59 / 48	73 / 67
Ethiopia	116	42.4 / 44.3	1,400	48 / 27	57 / 53
Kenya	66	51.1 / 53.0	650	85 / 85	60 / 62
Madagascar	83	56.0 / 59.0	660	92 / 91	49 / 33
Malawi	138	38.9 / 39.6	620	140 / 127	38 / 48
Mauritius (2)	16	67.9 / 75.1	112	107 / 106	98 / 99
Mozambique	114	43.9 / 46.6	1,500	70 / 50	52 / 39
Rwanda	124	39.4 / 41.7	1,300	83 / 80	58 / 60
Somalia	122	45.4 / 48.6			
Uganda	107	38.9 / 40.4	550	81 / 68	82 / 73
United Republic of Tanzania	82	46.8 / 49.1	530	67 / 66	81 / 85
Zambia	82	39.5 / 40.6	230	91 / 86	89 / 84
Zimbabwe	69	43.6 / 44.7	280	115 / 111	78 / 79
Middle Africa (3)	95	48.6 / 51.7			
Angola	125	44.9 / 48.1	1,500	96 / 88	
Cameroon	74	53.4 / 56.0	550	93 / 84	64 / 69
Central African Republic	98	42.9 / 46.9	700	69 / 45	39 / 32
Chad	112	45.7 / 48.7	900	76 / 39	62 / 53
Congo, Democratic Republic of (4)	90	49.2 / 52.3		86 / 59	68 / 58
Congo, Republic of	90	46.3 / 50.8	890	120 / 109	40 / 78
Gabon	87	51.1 / 53.8	500		58 / 61
Northern Africa (5)	52	63.3 / 66.4			
Algeria	44	67.5 / 70.3	140	113 / 102	94 / 95
Egypt	51	64.7 / 67.9	170	107 / 94	95 / 93
Libyan Arab Jamahiriya	28	68.3 / 72.2	220	110 / 111	
Morocco	51	64.8 / 68.5	372	97 / 74	79 / 77
Sudan	71	53.6 / 56.4	370	55 / 47	90 / 95
Tunisia	30	68.4 / 70.7		120 / 113	90 / 92
Southern Africa	62	51.5 / 57.5			
Botswana	59	46.2 / 48.4	250	107 / 108	87 / 93
Lesotho	93	54.7 / 57.3	610	102 / 114	72 / 87
Namibia	65	51.8 / 53.0	220	130 / 132	80 / 84
South Africa	59	51.5 / 58.1	230	133 / 129	72 / 79

Indicators of Education		Reproductive Health Indicators				
Secondary enrolment (gross)	% Illiterate (>15 years)	Contraceptive knowledge		Births per 1,000 women aged 15-19	Contraceptive prevalence	
M / F	M / F	% knowing method	% knowing source		Any method	Modern methods
				65	58	50
				31	70	51
				71	55	50
				128		
				119	20	16
				132		
8 / 5	48 / 67	70	62	55	9	1
24 / 17				119	5	4
13 / 10	60 / 74	63		152	4	2
26 / 22	14 / 31	96	88	95	33	28
16 / 16			45	137	17	5
21 / 12	28 / 59	90	80	162	22	14
63 / 66	14 / 22	100		37	75	49
9 / 6	46 / 77			128	6	6
12 / 9	31 / 48	98	86	56	21	13
				213		
15 / 9	26 / 50	82	74	180	15	8
6 / 5	20 / 41	74	66	125	18	13
34 / 21	18 / 35	89	81	134	25	14
52 / 45	7 / 14	96	93	89	48	42
				196		
18 / 9				219		
32 / 22	23 / 39	72	54	140	16	4
15 / 6	46 / 73			142	15	3
15 / 4				185		
32 / 19				217	8	2
62 / 45	17 / 33			141		
				172		
				50		
65 / 62	29 / 55	99		25	52	49
80 / 70	37 / 62	100	93	65	47	46
61 / 57	13 / 40			56	40	26
44 / 34	42 / 70	99	94	50	50	42
23 / 20	37 / 62	71	60	52	8	6
66 / 63	24 / 47	99	97	13	60	51
				71		
62 / 68	30 / 25	95	95	70	33	32
75 / 77	30 / 8	79		86	23	19
56 / 66	20 / 23	89	78	105	29	26
87 / 102	16 / 18			68	50	49

	Indicators of Mortality			Indicators of Education	
	Infant mortality Total per 1,000 live births	Life expectancy M / F	Maternal mortality ratio	Primary enrolment (gross) M / F	Proportion reaching grade 5 M / F
Western Africa (6)	**90**	**48.6 / 51.3**			
Benin	88	51.7 / 55.2	500	98 / 57	64 / 57
Burkina Faso	99	43.6 / 45.2	930	48 / 31	74 / 77
Côte d'Ivoire	87	46.2 / 47.3	600	82 / 61	77 / 71
Ghana	66	58.3 / 61.8	740	81 / 69	81 / 79
Guinea	124	46.0 / 47.0	880	62 / 33	85 / 68
Guinea-Bissau	130	43.5 / 46.5	910	79 / 45	
Liberia	116	46.1 / 48.5		51 / 28	
Mali	118	52.0 / 54.6	580	55 / 35	87 / 82
Mauritania	92	51.9 / 55.1	800	84 / 75	61 / 68
Niger	115	46.9 / 50.1	593	36 / 22	72 / 74
Nigeria	81	48.7 / 51.5	1,000	109 / 87	
Senegal	63	50.5 / 54.2	510	75 / 61	89 / 81
Sierra Leone	170	35.8 / 38.7	1,800	60 / 41	
Togo	84	47.6 / 50.1	640	140 / 99	74 / 58
Asia	**57**	**64.8 / 67.9**			
Eastern Asia (7)	**38**	**68.8 / 73.4**			
China	41	67.9 / 72.0	115	120 / 120	93 / 94
Democratic People's Republic of Korea	22	68.9 / 75.1			
Hong Kong, China (8)	6	75.8 / 81.4	7	93 / 95	99 / 100
Japan	4	76.8 / 82.9	8	102 / 102	100 / 100
Mongolia	51	64.4 / 67.3	65	86 / 91	
Republic of Korea	10	68.8 / 76.0	30	94 / 94	100 / 100
South Eastern Asia	**46**	**63.7 / 67.8**			
Cambodia	103	51.5 / 55.0	900	119 / 100	56 / 42
Indonesia	48	63.3 / 67.0	390	117 / 112	96 / 81
Lao People's Democratic Republic	93	52.0 / 54.5	650	123 / 101	55 / 51
Malaysia	11	69.9 / 74.3	43	101 / 103	98 / 100
Myanmar	79	58.5 / 61.8	580	122 / 117	
Philippines	36	66.5 / 70.2	208	109 / 110	75 / 75
Singapore	5	74.9 / 79.3	10	103 / 99	100 / 100
Thailand	29	65.8 / 72.0	200	98 / 96	
Viet Nam	38	64.9 / 69.6	105	106 / 100	
South Central Asia	**73**	**61.8 / 62.9**			
Afghanistan	152	45.0 / 46.0		64 / 32	86 / 80
Bangladesh	79	58.1 / 58.2	850	77 / 66	18 / 26
Bhutan	63	59.5 / 62.0			81 / 84
India	72	62.3 / 62.9	437	109 / 90	62 / 55
Iran (Islamic Republic of)	35	68.5 / 70.0	120	102 / 95	92 / 89
Nepal	83	57.6 / 57.1	1,500	127 / 90	52 / 52
Pakistan	74	62.9 / 65.1	340	101 / 45	
Sri Lanka	18	70.9 / 75.4	30	110 / 108	83 / 84

Indicators of Education		Reproductive Health Indicators				
Secondary enrolment (gross)	% Illiterate (>15 years)	Contraceptive knowledge		Births per 1,000 women aged 15-19	Contraceptive prevalence	
M / F	M / F	% knowing method	% knowing source		Any method	Modern methods
				136		
24 / 10	55 / 81	40		116	16	3
11 / 6	71 / 90	66	30	157	8	4
33 / 16	51 / 70	26		133	11	5
44 / 28	25 / 47	76	70	113	20	10
18 / 6				193	2	1
10 / 4	53 / 84			190		
31 / 13	38 / 72	72	48	213	6	5
13 / 7	60 / 75	42	30	181	7	5
21 / 11	51 / 73	61		135	3	1
9 / 5	80 / 93	76	33	199	4	2
36 / 30	34 / 53	46	34	121	6	3
20 / 12	57 / 77	74	44	119	13	8
22 / 13		78		202		
40 / 15	34 / 65	94	81	120	12	3
				57	60	56
				5		
73 / 66	10 / 27			5	83	83
				2	62	53
71 / 76	4 / 13	98		7	86	79
103 / 104				4	59	53
48 / 65				47	61	25
102 / 102	1 / 5	100	94	4	79	69
				48		
36 / 21				14		
52 / 44	10 / 22	95	93	58	55	52
35 / 23				104	19	15
57 / 65	11 / 21	99	94	25	48	31
29 / 30	12 / 22			26	17	14
77 / 78	6 / 6	97	93	43	40	25
69 / 65	5 / 14	98	95	7	74	73
57 / 56	4 / 8	100	99	70	74	72
48 / 46	5 / 12	95		27	65	44
				103		
32 / 12	54 / 84	4		153	2	2
25 / 13	51 / 74	100	98	115	49	41
				71	19	
59 / 39	35 / 62	95		112	41	77
81 / 73	21 / 37	91		74	65	45
50 / 30	47 / 81	93	80	120	29	26
33 / 17	46 / 76	78	46	90	18	13
72 / 78	6 / 13	99	98	20	66	43

111

	Indicators of Mortality			Indicators of Education	
	Infant mortality Total per 1,000 live births	Life expectancy M / F	Maternal mortality ratio	Primary enrolment (gross) M / F	Proportion reaching grade 5 M / F
Western Asia (9)	**51**	**65.9 / 70.2**			
Iraq	95	60.9 / 63.9	310	92 / 78	84 / 84
Israel	8	75.7 / 79.7	7	96 / 96	
Jordan	26	68.9 / 71.5	150		98 / 99
Kuwait	12	74.1 / 78.2	18	76 / 74	
Lebanon	29	68.1 / 71.7	300	113 / 108	
Oman	25	68.9 / 73.3		80 / 76	96 / 96
Saudi Arabia	23	69.9 / 73.4	18	77 / 75	87 / 92
Syrian Arab Republic	33	66.7 / 71.2	179	106 / 96	93 / 94
Turkey (10)	45	66.5 / 71.7	180	107 / 102	92 / 93
United Arab Emirates	16	73.9 / 76.5		96 / 92	98 / 98
Yemen	80	57.4 / 58.4	1,400	100 / 40	
Europe	**12**	**69.2 / 77.4**			
Eastern Europe	**18**	**63.3 / 73.9**			
Bulgaria	17	67.6 / 74.7	20	100 / 98	91 / 90
Czech Republic	6	70.3 / 77.4	7	105 / 103	
Hungary	10	66.8 / 74.9	14	104 / 102	98 / 98
Poland	15	68.2 / 76.9	10	97 / 96	
Romania	23	66.2 / 73.9	41	104 / 103	
Slovakia	11	69.2 / 76.7	8	102 / 102	
Northern Europe (11)	**8**	**73.5 / 79.5**			
Denmark	7	73.0 / 78.3	9	102 / 101	100 / 99
Estonia	19	63.0 / 74.5	52	95 / 93	96 / 97
Finland	6	73.0 / 80.6	11	99 / 99	100 / 100
Ireland	7	73.6 / 79.2	10	104 / 104	100 / 100
Latvia	18	62.5 / 74.4	15	98 / 93	
Lithuania	21	64.3 / 75.6	13	100 / 96	
Norway	5	75.2 / 81.1	6	99 / 99	100 / 100
Sweden	5	76.3 / 80.8	7	105 / 107	98 / 97
United Kingdom	7	74.5 / 79.8	9	114 / 116	
Southern Europe (12)	**10**	**73.7 / 80.1**			
Albania	30	69.9 / 75.9	28	106 / 108	81 / 83
Bosnia & Herzegovina	15	70.5 / 75.9			
Croatia	10	68.8 / 76.5	12	88 / 87	
Greece	8	75.6 / 80.7	10	94 / 94	99 / 100
Italy	7	75.0 / 81.2	12	101 / 100	100 / 100
Macedonia (The former Yugoslav Republic of)	23	70.9 / 75.3	22	100 / 98	95 / 95
Portugal	9	71.8 / 78.9	15	131 / 125	
Slovenia	7	70.6 / 78.2	5	98 / 98	
Spain	7	74.5 / 81.5	7	110 / 108	98 / 99
Yugoslavia	18	70.2 / 75.5	12	69 / 70	

Indicators of Education		Reproductive Health Indicators				
Secondary enrolment (gross)	% Illiterate (>15 years)	Contraceptive knowledge		Births per 1,000 women aged 15-19	Contraceptive prevalence	
M / F	M / F	% knowing method	% knowing source		Any method	Modern methods
				57		
51 / 33				45	14	11
89 / 87	3 / 7			19		
	10 / 20	100	95	43	35	27
65 / 65	18 / 24			34	35	32
78 / 85	10 / 23	91		26	53	18
68 / 65	25 / 49			80	22	19
65 / 57	20 / 41			113		
45 / 40	15 / 46	78		44	36	28
67 / 45	8 / 28	99	95	44	63	35
76 / 84	27 / 25			73	27	24
53 / 14	38 / 82	60	27	102	13	10
				25	**72**	**46**
				38		
77 / 77	1 / 3			49	76	7
97 / 100				23	69	45
96 / 99	1 / 1			28	73	59
98 / 97	0 / 0			23	75	26
79 / 78	1 / 4			36	57	14
92 / 96				32	74	42
				24		
120 / 123				9	78	71
100 / 108				38	70	56
107 / 125				10	80	77
112 / 120				19		
82 / 85	0 / 1			27	48	39
85 / 88	1 / 1			37	59	20
119 / 113				13	74	69
126 / 148				7	78	71
123 / 144				29	82	78
				14		
37 / 38				34		
				28		
81 / 83	1 / 4			19		
95 / 96	2 / 6			13		
94 / 94	1 / 2			7	78	32
64 / 62				42		
102 / 111	7 / 13			20	66	32
90 / 93	0 / 1			17		
116 / 128	2 / 4			8	59	37
60 / 64				39	55	12

Monitoring ICPD Goals — Selected Indicators

	Indicators of Mortality			Indicators of Education	
	Infant mortality Total per 1,000 live births	Life expectancy M / F	Maternal mortality ratio	Primary enrolment (gross) M / F	Proportion reaching grade 5 M / F
Western Europe (13)	**6**	**74.1 / 80.8**			
Austria	6	73.7 / 80.2	10	101 / 101	
Belgium	7	73.8 / 80.6	10	103 / 102	
France	6	74.2 / 82.0	15	107 / 105	
Germany	5	73.9 / 80.2	22	102 / 102	
Netherlands	6	75.0 / 80.7	12	108 / 106	93 / 96
Switzerland	6	75.4 / 81.8	6		
Latin America & Caribbean	**36**	**66.1 / 72.6**			
Caribbean (14)	**36**	**66.3 / 71.0**			
Cuba	9	74.2 / 78.0	36	108 / 104	
Dominican Republic	34	69.0 / 73.1	110	103 / 104	
Haiti	68	51.4 / 56.2	600	49 / 46	47 / 46
Jamaica	22	72.9 / 76.8	120	100 / 99	93 / 98
Puerto Rico	12	69.4 / 78.5			
Trinidad & Tobago	15	71.5 / 76.2	90	99 / 98	98 / 99
Central America	**33**	**68.4 / 74.0**			
Belize	29	73.4 / 76.1		123 / 119	70 / 71
Costa Rica	12	74.3 / 78.9	55	104 / 103	86 / 89
El Salvador	32	66.5 / 72.5	300	93 / 92	76 / 77
Guatemala	46	61.4 / 67.2	190	94 / 82	52 / 47
Honduras	35	67.5 / 72.3	220	110 / 112	45 / 51
Mexico	31	69.5 / 75.5	110	116 / 113	85 / 86
Nicaragua	43	65.8 / 70.6	160	101 / 104	52 / 57
Panama	21	71.8 / 76.4	55	108 / 104	80 / 84
South America (15)	**37**	**65.3 / 72.3**			
Argentina	22	69.7 / 76.8	100	114 / 113	
Bolivia	66	59.8 / 63.2	370	99 / 90	63 / 58
Brazil	42	63.1 / 71.0	160	107 / 98	
Chile	13	72.3 / 78.3	180	103 / 100	100 / 100
Colombia	30	67.3 / 74.3	100	113 / 112	70 / 76
Ecuador	46	67.3 / 72.5	150	123 / 122	84 / 86
Paraguay	39	67.5 / 72.0	190	113 / 110	70 / 73
Peru	45	65.9 / 70.9	280	125 / 121	78 / 74
Uruguay	18	70.5 / 78.0	85	109 / 108	97 / 99
Venezuela	21	70.0 / 75.7	200	90 / 93	86 / 92
Northern America (16)	**7**	**73.6 / 80.2**			
Canada	6	76.1 / 81.8	6	103 / 101	
United States of America	7	73.4 / 80.1	12	103 / 101	

Indicators of Education		Reproductive Health Indicators				
Secondary enrolment (gross)	% Illiterate (>15 years)	Contraceptive knowledge		Births per 1,000 women aged 15-19	Contraceptive prevalence	
		% knowing method	% knowing source		Any method	Modern methods
M / F	M / F					
				10		
106 / 102				18	71	56
141 / 152				11	79	75
112 / 111				9	75	70
105 / 103				11	75	72
141 / 134				4	79	76
				4	71	65
				76	**66**	**57**
				74		
76 / 85	4 / 4	100		65	70	68
34 / 47	18 / 19	100	96	89	64	60
21 / 20	53 / 59	81	66	70	18	13
63 / 67	20 / 11	99		91	62	58
	7 / 7			70	64	57
72 / 75	2 / 3	97	96	40	53	45
				81		
47 / 52		95		99	47	42
45 / 50	5 / 5	100	99	85	75	65
32 / 36	21 / 27	98		95	53	48
27 / 25	27 / 43	70	64	119	31	26
29 / 37	30 / 31	95		115	50	41
61 / 61	8 / 13	91	72	70	67	58
41 / 47	37 / 37	97		152	49	45
61 / 65	9 / 10	95		82	58	54
				73		
73 / 81	4 / 4			65		
40 / 34	10 / 25	73	66	79	45	17
31 / 36	17 / 17	100	95	72	77	71
72 / 78	5 / 5			49		
65 / 69	10 / 10	98	94	88	72	59
50 / 50	8 / 12	89	88	72	57	46
42 / 45	7 / 10	98	90	76	56	41
72 / 67	7 / 17	96	89	58	64	41
75 / 90	3 / 2			70		
33 / 46	8 / 9	98	68	98	49	37
				56	**71**	**68**
105 / 105				23	75	74
98 / 97				59	71	67

	Indicators of Mortality			Indicators of Education	
	Infant mortality Total per 1,000 live births	Life expectancy M / F	Maternal mortality ratio	Primary enrolment (gross) M / F	Proportion reaching grade 5 M / F
Oceania	**24**	**71.4 / 76.3**			
Australia-New Zealand	6	75.2 / 80.9			
Australia (17)	6	75.5 / 81.1	9	101 / 101	
Melanesia (18)	53	59.9 / 62.2			
New Caledonia	11	69.2 / 76.3		127 / 123	96 / 94
New Zealand	7	74.1 / 79.7	25	99 / 99	99 / 99
Papua New Guinea	61	57.2 / 58.7	930	87 / 74	72 / 74
Vanuatu	39	65.5 / 69.5		101 / 94	90 / 91
Countries with Economies in Transition of the Former USSR (19)					
Armenia	26	67.2 / 73.6	21	87 / 91	
Azerbaijan	36	65.5 / 74.1	44	108 / 105	
Belarus	23	62.2 / 73.9	22	100 / 96	
Georgia	20	68.5 / 76.8	19	89 / 88	
Kazakhstan	35	62.8 / 72.5	53	97 / 98	
Kyrgyzstan	40	63.3 / 71.9	32	106 / 103	
Republic of Moldova	29	63.5 / 71.5	33	98 / 97	
Russian Federation	18	60.6 / 72.8	53	108 / 107	
Tajikistan	57	64.2 / 70.2	74	97 / 94	
Turkmenistan	55	61.9 / 68.9	44		
Ukraine	19	63.8 / 73.7	30	87 / 87	
Uzbekistan	44	64.3 / 70.7	24	79 / 77	

Indicators of Education		Reproductive Health Indicators				
Secondary enrolment (gross)	% Illiterate (>15 years)	Contraceptive knowledge		Births per 1,000 women	Contraceptive prevalence	
		% knowing method	% knowing source	aged 15-19	Any method	Modern methods
M / F	M / F					
				28	29	22
				22	76	72
149 / 148				20	76	72
				34		
80 / 88				55		
111 / 117				34	75	72
17 / 11				24	26	20
23 / 18				74		
100 / 79				41		
73 / 81				17		
91 / 95	0 / 2			36	50	42
78 / 76				47		
82 / 91				54	59	46
75 / 83				40		
79 / 82	1 / 3			32	74	50
84 / 91	0 / 2			45		
83 / 74	1 / 2			35		
				20		
88 / 95				36		
100 / 88				35	56	52

Demographic, Social and Economic Indicators

	Total population (millions) (1999)	Projected population (millions) (2025)	Avg. pop. growth rate (%) (1995-2000)	% urban (1995)	Urban growth rate (1995-2000)	Population/ ha arable and perm. crop land
World Total	**5,978.4**	**7,823.7**	**1.3**	**45**	**2.5**	
More-developed regions (*)	**1,185.2**	**1,214.9**	**0.3**	**75**	**0.7**	
Less-developed regions (+)	**4,793.2**	**6,608.8**	**1.6**	**38**	**3.3**	
Least-developed countries (‡)	**629.6**	**1,092.6**	**2.4**	**22**	**5.2**	
Africa (1)	**766.6**	**1,298.3**	**2.4**	**34**	**4.3**	
Eastern Africa	**240.9**	**426.2**	**2.6**	**22**	**5.3**	
Burundi	6.6	11.6	1.7	8	6.4	5.1
Eritrea	3.7	6.7	3.8	17	4.7	5.0
Ethiopia	61.1	115.4	2.5	13	5.1	4.1
Kenya	29.5	41.8	2.0	28	5.6	4.7
Madagascar	15.5	29.0	3.0	27	5.6	3.8
Malawi	10.6	20.0	2.4	14	4.6	4.6
Mauritius (2)	1.2	1.4	0.8	41	1.6	1.4
Mozambique	19.3	30.6	2.5	34	7.1	4.3
Rwanda	7.2	12.4	7.7	6	4.7	4.3
Somalia	9.7	21.2	4.2	26	4.7	7.0
Uganda	21.1	44.4	2.8	13	5.4	2.4
United Republic of Tanzania	32.8	57.9	2.3	24	5.7	6.2
Zambia	9.0	15.6	2.3	43	3.3	1.1
Zimbabwe	11.5	15.1	1.4	32	4.4	2.3
Middle Africa (3)	**93.2**	**184.7**	**2.7**	**33**	**4.5**	
Angola	12.5	25.1	3.2	32	5.6	2.3
Cameroon	14.7	26.5	2.7	45	4.7	1.1
Central African Republic	3.6	5.7	1.9	39	3.5	1.3
Chad	7.5	13.9	2.6	21	4.1	1.6
Congo, Democratic Republic of (4)	50.3	104.8	2.6	29	4.3	3.9
Congo, Republic of	2.9	5.7	2.8	59	4.2	6.9
Gabon	1.2	2.0	2.6	50	4.2	1.0
Northern Africa (5)	**170.0**	**249.1**	**2.0**	**46**	**3.1**	
Algeria	30.8	46.6	2.3	56	3.5	0.9
Egypt	67.2	95.6	1.9	45	2.6	7.6
Libyan Arab Jamahiriya	5.5	8.6	2.4	86	3.9	0.2
Morocco	27.9	38.7	1.8	48	2.9	1.1
Sudan	28.9	46.3	2.1	25	4.7	1.4
Tunisia	9.5	12.8	1.4	57	2.6	0.5
Southern Africa	**46.3**	**55.9**	**1.6**	**48**	**3.3**	
Botswana	1.6	2.2	1.9	28	6.3	1.9
Lesotho	2.1	3.5	2.2	23	5.8	2.5
Namibia	1.7	2.3	2.2	37	5.3	1.0
South Africa	39.9	46.0	1.5	51	3.0	0.4

Total fertility rate (1995-2000)	% births with skilled attendants	GNP per capita PPP$ (1995)	Per capita central govt. expenditures (PPP$) Education	Health	External population assistance (US$,000)	Under-5 mortality M / F	Per capita energy consumption	Access to safe water
2.71	58				(1,646,074)	80 / 80		
1.57	99					13 / 10		
3.00	53					87 / 88		
5.05						160 / 151		
5.06	42				464,557 [20]	146 / 133		
5.79	34					169 / 154		
6.28	24	620	19.2		5,530	189 / 168		58
5.70	21	1,040	18.7		4,459	154 / 137		7
6.30	8	500	20.0	8.0	29,130	193 / 174	284	26
4.45	45	1,160	76.6	18.0	29,270	107 / 101	476	45
5.40	57	900	17.1		11,162	123 / 110		16
6.75	55	700	38.5		22,695	223 / 217		60
1.91	97	9,230	396.9	172.0	324	22 / 13		100
6.25	44	690			22,207	193 / 173	481	24
6.20	26	650			5,586	213 / 191		
7.25	2				2,906	212 / 195		
7.10	38	1,160	30.2	16.2	31,133	181 / 164		42
5.48	38	620			35,037	138 / 123	453	49
5.55	47	910	20.0	24.6	19,954	149 / 144	628	53
3.80	69	2,240	185.9	47.9	23,301	123 / 111	929	77
6.17	42					158 / 139		
6.80	17	820			5,443	217 / 199	532	32
5.30	58	1,770	51.3	17.5	6,647	120 / 109	369	41
4.90	46	1,310			2,546	172 / 141		23
6.07	15	950	22.8	31.9	4,024	184 / 164		24
6.43		760			1,945	148 / 130	305	
6.06	50	1,290	80.0	42.1	1,021	147 / 116	457	
5.40	80	6,560	183.7		677	143 / 127	1,403	67
3.58	64				80,806 [21]	73 / 67		
3.81	77	4,250	216.8	152.1	1,354	57 / 45	842	
3.40	46	3,080	147.8	45.9	36,154	65 / 64	638	84
3.80	94				11	32 / 31	2,935	95
3.10	40	3,210	170.1	41.2	31,766	74 / 62	329	57
4.61	86	1,370			3,931	115 / 108	397	60
2.55	81	5,050	338.4	133.9	3,751	38 / 36	735	90
3.43	79					102 / 82		
4.?5	77	7,180	112.7		2,505	113 / 101		70
4.75	50	2,490	174.3		1,050	132 / 127		62
4.90	68	5,100	464.1	171.2	2,265	125 / 119		60
3.25	82	7,190	568.0	246.6	20,540	98 / 76	2,482	59

Demographic, Social and Economic Indicators

	Total population (millions) (1999)	Projected population (millions) (2025)	Avg. pop. growth rate (%) (1995-2000)	% urban (1995)	Urban growth rate (1995-2000)	Population/ ha arable and perm. crop land
Western Africa (6)	**216.3**	**382.5**	**2.5**	**37**	**4.9**	
Benin	5.9	11.1	2.7	31	4.6	1.7
Burkina Faso	11.6	23.3	2.7	27	8.9	2.9
Côte d'Ivoire	14.5	23.3	1.8	44	4.7	1.0
Ghana	19.7	36.9	2.7	36	4.4	2.3
Guinea	7.4	12.5	0.8	30	5.5	7.2
Guinea-Bissau	1.2	1.9	2.2	22	4.6	2.7
Liberia	2.9	6.6	8.2	45	4.5	4.8
Mali	11.0	21.3	2.4	27	5.4	2.0
Mauritania	2.6	4.8	2.7	54	4.3	2.5
Niger	10.4	21.5	3.2	17	5.8	1.7
Nigeria	108.9	183.0	2.4	39	4.8	1.3
Senegal	9.2	16.7	2.6	42	4.0	2.8
Sierra Leone	4.7	8.1	3.0	36	4.4	5.1
Togo	4.5	8.5	2.6	31	4.8	1.1
Asia	**3,634.3**	**4,723.1**	**1.4**	**35**	**3.2**	
Eastern Asia (7)	**1,473.4**	**1,695.4**	**0.9**	**37**	**2.9**	
China	1,266.8	1,480.4	0.9	30	3.6	6.3
Democratic People's Republic of Korea	23.7	29.4	1.6	61	2.3	3.7
Hong Kong, China (8)	6.8	7.7	2.1	95	0.5	5.1
Japan	126.5	121.2	0.2	78	0.4	1.5
Mongolia	2.6	3.7	1.7	61	2.9	0.5
Republic of Korea	46.5	52.5	0.8	81	2.1	2.6
South Eastern Asia	**511.1**	**683.5**	**1.5**	**34**	**3.7**	
Cambodia	10.9	16.5	2.3	21	5.6	1.9
Indonesia	209.3	273.4	1.4	35	4.1	3.0
Lao People's Democratic Republic	5.3	9.7	2.6	22	5.7	4.6
Malaysia	21.8	31.0	2.0	54	3.4	0.6
Myanmar	45.1	58.1	1.2	26	3.7	3.2
Philippines	74.5	108.3	2.1	54	3.7	3.0
Singapore	3.5	4.2	1.4	100	0.8	7.0
Thailand	60.9	72.7	0.9	20	2.8	1.5
Viet Nam	78.7	108.0	1.6	21	3.5	7.7
South Central Asia	**1,465.8**	**2,049.9**	**1.8**	**29**	**3.4**	
Afghanistan	21.9	44.9	2.9	20	7.7	1.8
Bangladesh	126.9	178.8	1.7	18	5.2	8.1
Bhutan	2.1	3.9	2.8	6	6.3	11.3
India	998.1	1,330.4	1.6	27	3.0	3.2
Iran (Islamic Republic of)	66.8	94.5	1.7	59	3.0	1.1
Nepal	23.4	38.0	2.4	14	6.5	6.9
Pakistan	152.3	263.0	2.8	35	4.6	3.4
Sri Lanka	18.6	23.5	1.0	22	2.8	4.6

Total fertility rate (1995-2000)	% births with skilled attendants	GNP per capita PPP$ (1995)	Per capita central govt. expenditures (PPP$) Education	Health	External population assistance (US$,000)	Under-5 mortality M / F	Per capita energy consumption	Access to safe water
5.47	**35**					**162 / 149**		
5.80	60	1,260	40.3		5,808	142 / 124	341	72
6.57	41	1,000	15.0	29.2	9,133	176 / 166		
5.10	45	1,690	84.5	23.2	8,279	144 / 129	382	72
5.15	44	1,610		30.3	16,050	107 / 95	380	65
5.51	31	1,790			10,443	207 / 208		55
5.75	25				1,802	214 / 192		53
6.31	58				934	184 / 163		
6.60	24	720	15.8	9.5	12,779	244 / 227		
5.50	40	1,650	84.2	24.9	1,045	155 / 142		64
6.84	15	830			6,473	198 / 181		48
5.15	31	860	7.7	2.4	18,678	154 / 140	722	50
5.57	47	1,690	59.2		9,571	117 / 112	302	50
6.06	25	410			400	277 / 248		34
6.05	32	1,460	68.6	24.6	2,073	137 / 120		55
2.60	**54**				**371,539**	**71 / 77**		
1.77	**86**					**39 / 50**		
1.80	85	3,070	70.6	49.1	4,701	43 / 54	902	83
2.05	100				2,337	27 / 25	1,063	100
1.32	100	24,350	706.2	525.5	19	8 / 6	1,931	
1.43	100	24,400	878.4	1,284.9	(93,760) [22]	6 / 5	4,058	96
2.60	99	1,490	95.4	74.7	971	72 / 75		54
1.65	95	13,430	496.9	299.6	119	13 / 13	3,576	83
2.69	**54**					**66 / 57**		
4.60	31	1,290	37.4		19,756	141 / 127		13
2.58	36	3,390	47.5	20.0	32,553	69 / 56	672	65
5.75	30	1,300	32.5	15.0	3,409	154 / 146		51
3.18	98	7,730	402.0	150.4	843	16 / 13	1,950	89
2.40	57				884	121 / 104	294	60
3.62	53	3,670	80.7	37.7	48,602	49 / 38	528	83
1.68	100	29,230	876.9	364.4	8	6 / 6	7,835	100
1.74	71	6,490	266.1	116.9	10,181	37 / 33	1,333	89
2.60	79	1,590	41.3	13.7	17,113	54 / 57	448	47
3.36	**34**					**91 / 101**		
6.90	8				1,060	257 / 257		
3.11	8	1,090	31.6	11.3	93,492	106 / 116	197	84
5.50	12				1,076	98 / 94		
3.13	35	1,660	56.4	8.8	46,228	82 / 97	476	85
2.80	74	5,690	227.6	85.0	1,791	52 / 51	1,491	90
4.45	9	1,090	30.5	12.6	17,323	110 / 124	320	59
5.03	18	1,580	47.4	10.7	16,722	108 / 104	446	62
2.10	94	2,460	83.6	28.8	2,186	22 / 20	371	70

Demographic, Social and Economic Indicators

	Total population (millions) (1999)	Projected population (millions) (2025)	Avg. pop. growth rate (%) (1995-2000)	% urban (1995)	Urban growth rate (1995-2000)	Population/ ha arable and perm. crop land
Western Asia (9)	**184.0**	**294.3**	**2.2**	**66**	**3.4**	
Iraq	22.5	41.0	2.8	75	3.7	0.4
Israel	6.1	8.3	2.2	91	1.6	0.4
Jordan	6.5	12.1	3.0	71	4.1	1.4
Kuwait	1.9	3.0	3.1	97	3.4	3.4
Lebanon	3.2	4.4	1.7	87	2.3	0.5
Oman	2.5	5.4	3.3	13	7.4	14.4
Saudi Arabia	20.9	40.0	3.4	80	3.9	0.6
Syrian Arab Republic	15.7	26.3	2.5	52	4.3	0.8
Turkey (10)	65.5	87.9	1.7	69	3.5	0.8
United Arab Emirates	2.4	3.3	2.0	84	2.5	1.8
Yemen	17.5	39.0	3.7	34	5.9	5.5
Europe	**728.9**	**702.3**	**0.0**	**74**	**0.5**	
Eastern Europe	**307.6**	**287.5**	**-0.2**	**70**	**0.5**	
Bulgaria	8.3	7.0	-0.7	71	0.3	0.2
Czech Republic	10.3	9.5	-0.2	65	0.4	0.3
Hungary	10.1	8.9	-0.4	65	0.4	0.3
Poland	38.7	39.1	0.1	65	0.9	0.6
Romania	22.4	19.9	-0.4	55	0.6	0.4
Slovakia	5.4	5.4	0.1	59	1.2	0.3
Northern Europe (11)	**94.3**	**95.9**	**0.2**	**84**	**0.4**	
Denmark	5.3	5.2	0.3	85	0.2	0.1
Estonia	1.4	1.1	-1.2	73	-0.1	0.2
Finland	5.2	5.3	0.3	63	1.0	0.1
Ireland	3.7	4.4	0.7	58	0.8	0.3
Latvia	2.4	1.9	-1.5	73	-0.2	0.2
Lithuania	3.7	3.4	-0.3	72	0.7	0.2
Norway	4.4	4.8	0.5	73	0.7	0.3
Sweden	8.9	9.1	0.3	83	0.5	0.1
United Kingdom	58.7	60.0	0.2	89	0.4	0.2
Southern Europe (12)	**144.1**	**135.0**	**0.1**	**65**	**0.6**	
Albania	3.1	3.8	-0.4	37	2.2	2.5
Bosnia & Herzegovina	3.8	4.3	3.0	49	6.1	0.4
Croatia	4.5	4.2	-0.1	64	0.9	0.4
Greece	10.6	9.9	0.3	65	1.0	0.4
Italy	57.3	51.3	0.0	67	0.2	0.3
Macedonia (The former Yugoslav Republic of)	2.0	2.3	0.6	60	1.5	0.5
Portugal	9.9	9.3	0.0	36	1.4	0.6
Slovenia	2.0	1.8	-0.1	64	1.2	0.2
Spain	39.6	36.7	0.0	76	0.4	0.2
Yugoslavia	10.6	10.8	0.1	57	0.9	0.6

Total fertility rate (1995-2000)	% births with skilled attendants	GNP per capita PPP$ (1995)	Per capita central govt. expenditures (PPP$)		External population assistance (US$,000)	Under-5 mortality M / F	Per capita energy consumption	Access to safe water
			Education	Health				
3.77	74				34,462 [21]	69 / 61		
5.25	54				481	119 / 114	1,174	77
2.68	99	17,680	1,273.0	325.5	28	11 / 9	2,843	99
4.86	97	3,350	244.6	121.8	7,897	32 / 31	1,040	98
2.89	98				304	16 / 14	8,167	100
2.69	89	6,090	152.3		608	39 / 31	1,164	94
5.85	91				352	35 / 24	2,231	88
5.80	90	10,540	579.7	176.9		31 / 24	4,753	93
4.00	77	3,000	126.0		2,678	47 / 33	1,002	88
2.50	76	6,470	142.3	161.4	7,205	67 / 52	1,045	
3.42	99			316.0		21 / 17	13,155	98
7.60	43	720	46.8	4.1	10,528	112 / 114	187	39
1.42	99					16 / 12		
1.36	99				22,533 [21,23]	25 / 18		
1.23	100	3,870	127.7	205.1	362	23 / 16	2,705	
1.19	99	10,380	560.5	741.3	3	9 / 7	3,917	
1.37	99	6,970	327.6	317.2	78	13 / 10	2,499	
1.53	99	6,510	338.5	276.3	226	18 / 14	2,807	
1.17	99	4,270	153.7		2,740	39 / 26	2,027	62
1.39	95	7,860	385.1			14 / 12	3,266	
1.69	99					10 / 8		
1.72	100	23,450	1,922.9	1,176.2	(46,990)	10 / 7	4,346	
1.29	95	5,090	371.6			33 / 17	3,834	
1.73	100	19,660	1,494.2	1,085.1	(17,335)	7 / 6	6,143	98
1.90	99	17,420	1,010.4	998.1		9 / 7	3,293	
1.25	98	3,970	258.1		768	31 / 18	1,674	
1.43	95	4,140	231.8		24	29 / 18	2,414	
1.85	100	24,260	1,819.5	1,515.2	(54,296)	7 / 6	5,284	100
1.57	100	19,010	1,577.8	1,415.8	(53,177)	7 / 6	5,944	
1.72	98	20,710	1,118.3	1,171.5	(11,431)	9 / 8	3,992	100
1.31	98					13 / 11		
2.50	99	2,170	67.3		1,426	46 / 39	362	76
1.35	97				635	19 / 15	777	
1.56		4,930	261.3	346.1	116	14 / 11	1,418	63
1.28	99	12,540	376.2	630.9		9 / 8	2,328	
1.20	100	20,100	944.7	1,111.4	(2,203)	9 / 8	2,808	
2.06	93	3,180	178.1			27 / 24		
1.37	98	14,180	779.9	668.2	(414)	12 / 10	1,928	82
1.26	100	11,880	689.0			9 / 8	3,098	98
1.15	96	15,690	768.8	903.1	(7,438)	9 / 7	2,583	
1.84					18	28 / 23	1,364	

Demographic, Social and Economic Indicators

	Total population (millions) (1999)	Projected population (millions) (2025)	Avg. pop. growth rate (%) (1995-2000)	% urban (1995)	Urban growth rate (1995-2000)	Population/ ha arable and perm. crop land
Western Europe (13)	**183.0**	**183.9**	**0.3**	**81**	**0.4**	
Austria	8.2	8.2	0.5	56	0.7	0.3
Belgium	10.2	9.9	0.1	97	0.3	0.3 [24]
France	58.9	61.7	0.4	73	0.5	0.1
Germany	82.2	80.2	0.1	87	0.3	0.2
Netherlands	15.7	15.8	0.4	89	0.6	0.6
Switzerland	7.3	7.6	0.7	61	1.3	1.2
Latin America & Caribbean	**511.3**	**696.7**	**1.6**	**74**	**2.3**	
Caribbean (14)	**37.7**	**47.3**	**1.1**	**62**	**2.0**	
Cuba	11.2	11.8	0.4	76	1.2	0.4
Dominican Republic	8.4	11.2	1.7	65	2.7	0.9
Haiti	8.1	12.0	1.7	32	4.1	5.2
Jamaica	2.6	3.2	0.9	54	1.7	2.3
Puerto Rico	3.8	4.5	0.8	73	1.4	2.4
Trinidad & Tobago	1.3	1.5	0.5	72	1.8	1.0
Central America	**132.8**	**188.5**	**1.9**	**68**	**2.6**	
Belize	0.2	0.4	2.4	47	2.6	0.8
Costa Rica	3.9	5.9	2.5	50	3.2	1.5
El Salvador	6.2	9.1	2.0	45	2.9	2.4
Guatemala	11.1	19.8	2.6	41	4.1	3.0
Honduras	6.3	10.7	2.8	44	4.3	1.1
Mexico	97.4	130.2	1.6	75	2.4	0.9
Nicaragua	4.9	8.7	2.7	63	4.0	0.4
Panama	2.8	3.8	1.6	53	2.4	1.0
South America (15)	**340.8**	**460.9**	**1.5**	**78**	**2.2**	
Argentina	36.6	47.2	1.3	88	1.5	0.1
Bolivia	8.1	13.1	2.3	61	3.8	1.5
Brazil	168.0	217.9	1.3	78	2.3	0.5
Chile	15.0	19.5	1.4	84	1.6	0.6
Colombia	41.6	59.8	1.9	73	2.2	1.9
Ecuador	12.4	17.8	2.0	58	3.1	1.2
Paraguay	5.4	9.4	2.6	53	3.8	0.9
Peru	25.2	35.5	1.7	72	2.5	1.8
Uruguay	3.3	3.9	0.7	90	0.8	0.3
Venezuela	23.7	34.8	2.0	93	2.4	0.7
Northern America (16)	**307.2**	**363.6**	**0.9**	**76**	**1.2**	
Canada	30.9	37.9	1.0	77	1.2	0.0
United States of America	276.2	325.6	0.8	76	1.2	0.0

Total fertility rate (1995-2000)	% births with skilled attendants	GNP per capita PPP$ (1995)	Per capita central govt. expenditures (PPP$) Education	Health	External population assistance (US$,000)	Under-5 mortality M / F	Per capita energy consumption	Access to safe water
1.48	**100**					**8 / 6**		
1.41	100	22,010	1,232.6	1,256.5	(577)	8 / 7	3,373	
1.55	100	23,090	738.9	1,530.7	(9,814)	9 / 7	5,552	
1.71	99	22,210	1,354.8	1,636.8	(16,500)	8 / 7	4,355	100
1.30	100	21,170	1,016.2	1,730.2	(122,462) [25]	7 / 6	4,267	
1.50	100	21,300	1,107.6	1,285.6	(146,428)	9 / 7	4,885	99
1.47	99	26,580	1,408.7	1,766.1	(16,626)	10 / 7	3,622	100
2.70	**80**				**210,449**	**49 / 39**		
2.55	**72**					**57 / 48**		
1.55	99				935	13 / 10	1,448	91
2.80	96	4,690	93.8	71.4	6,789	51 / 41	652	73
4.38	20	1,260		15.1	16,296	112 / 97	268	39
2.50	92	3,330	246.4	89.9	5,088	28 / 25	1,465	93
2.11	99					15 / 13		97
1.65	98	6,460	239.0	129.3	59	19 / 12	6,081	96
3.05	**70**					**45 / 38**		
3.66	79	4,080			79	37 / 37		
2.83	97	6,510	345.0	398.3	748	16 / 13	657	100
3.17	87	2,860	62.9	63.1	5,872	45 / 37	700	53
4.93	35	4,060	69.0	58.7	5,568	65 / 57	510	67
4.30	55	2,260	81.4	52.7	7,422	54 / 43	503	77
2.75	75	8,110	397.4	216.5	23,326	41 / 34	1,525	95
4.42	61	1,820	67.3	106.1	11,529	64 / 53	525	62
2.63	84	6,890	316.9	320.3	388	29 / 26	853	84
2.58	**86**					**50 / 39**		
2.62	97	10,100	353.5	413.9	1,652	28 / 22	1,673	65
4.36	46	2,810	157.4	112.4	21,718	92 / 83	479	70
2.27	88	6,350	349.3	105.8	20,919	54 / 41	1,012	69
2.44	99	12,240	379.4	300.3	4,760	17 / 13	1,419	91
2.80	85	6,570	289.1	189.4	2,573	43 / 35	799	75
3.10	64	4,700	164.5	99.7	5,446	66 / 54	731	55
4.17	61	3,860	150.5	62.1	1,994	54 / 43	865	39
2.98	56	4,580	132.8	93.2	29,755	71 / 58	582	66
2.40	96	9,110	300.6	138.4	339	23 / 17	912	89
2.98	97	8,660	450.3	111.8	758	27 / 22	2,463	79
1.94	**99**					**9 / 7**		
1.55	100	21,750	1,522.5	1,451.9	(34,520)	8 / 6	7,880	99
1.99	99	29,080	1,570.3	1,844.1	(662,360)	10 / 8	8,051	73

Demographic, Social and Economic Indicators

	Total population (millions) (1999)	Projected population (millions) (2025)	Avg. pop. growth rate (%) (1995-2000)	% urban (1995)	Urban growth rate (1995-2000)	Population/ ha arable and perm. crop land
Oceania	**30.0**	**39.6**	**1.3**	**70**	**1.4**	
Australia-New Zealand	**22.5**	**27.8**	**1.0**	**85**	**1.2**	
Australia (17)	18.7	23.1	1.0	85	1.2	0.0
Melanesia (18)	6.3	10.0	2.2	21	3.6	
New Caledonia	0.2	0.3	2.1	62	2.2	
New Zealand	3.8	4.7	1.0	86	1.3	0.1
Papua New Guinea	4.7	7.5	2.2	16	4.0	6.4
Vanuatu	0.2	0.3	2.4	19	3.9	
Countries with Economies in Transition of the Former USSR (19)						
Armenia	3.5	3.9	-0.3	69	1.6	0.8
Azerbaijan	7.7	9.4	0.5	56	1.7	1.1
Belarus	10.3	9.5	-0.3	71	0.8	0.3
Georgia	5.0	5.2	-1.1	58	1.1	1.1
Kazakhstan	16.3	17.7	-0.4	60	1.4	0.1
Kyrgyzstan	4.7	6.1	0.6	39	2.4	0.9
Republic of Moldova	4.4	4.5	0.0	52	1.8	0.5
Russian Federation	147.2	137.9	-0.2	76	0.3	0.1
Tajikistan	6.1	8.9	1.5	32	3.2	2.4
Turkmenistan	4.4	6.3	1.8	45	2.5	1.0
Ukraine	50.7	45.7	-0.4	70	0.6	0.3
Uzbekistan	23.9	33.4	1.6	41	2.8	1.4

Total fertility rate (1995-2000)	% births with skilled attendants	GNP per capita PPP$ (1995)	Per capita central govt. expenditures (PPP$) Education	Health	External population assistance (US$,000)	Under-5 mortality M / F	Per capita energy consumption	Access to safe water
2.38	**65**					**31 / 32**		
1.83	**99**					**8 / 6**		
1.79	100	19,510	1,092.6	1,227.3	(45,235)	8 / 6	5,494	99
4.28						68 / 73		
2.70	98					16 / 15		
2.01	95	15,780	1,151.9	1,012.9	(1,806)	9 / 8	4,388	90
4.60	53					5,158	79 / 88		31
4.30	79	3,230			202	54 / 42		
1.70	95	2,540	50.8	61.8	2,040	35 / 30	474	
1.99	99	1,520	50.2	16.6	1,247	55 / 44	1,570	
1.36	100	4,820	294.0	222.7	25	36 / 20	2,386	
1.92	95	1,980	103.0		1,018	27 / 20	291	
2.30	99	3,530	165.9	81.7	1,270	46 / 36	2,724	
3.21	98	2,180	124.3		1,730	56 / 44	645	81
1.76	95	1,450	140.7		583	39 / 25	1,064	56
1.35	99	4,280	175.5	225.9	6,783	25 / 19	4,169	
4.15	92	1,100	24.2		943	88 / 73	594	69
3.60	90	1,410			1,012	86 / 69	2,646	60
1.38	100	2,170	156.2		1,956	30 / 20	3,012	55
3.45	98				2,849	69 / 56	1,826	57

Selected Indicators for Less-Populous Countries/Territories

Monitoring ICPD Goals — Selected Indicators

	Indicators of Mortality		Indicators of Education		Reproductive Health Indicators		
	Infant mortality Total per 1,000 live births	Life expectancy M / F	Primary enrolment (gross) M / F	Secondary enrolment (gross) M / F	Births per 1,000 women aged 15-19	Contraceptive prevalence Any method	Modern method
Bahamas	16	70.5 / 77.1	92 / 104	77 / 97	69	62	60
Bahrain	17	71.1 / 75.3	105 / 106	95 / 100	22	61	30
Barbados	12	73.7 / 78.7	90 / 91	89 / 80	44	55	53
Brunei Darussalam	10	73.4 / 78.1	109 / 104	72 / 82	33		
Cape Verde	56	65.5 / 71.3	133 / 129	28 / 26	79		
Comoros	76	57.4 / 60.2	84 / 69	24 / 19	83	21	11
Cyprus	9	75.5 / 80.0	100 / 100	96 / 99	17		
Djibouti	106	48.7 / 52.0	45 / 33	17 / 12	31		
East Timor	135	46.7 / 48.4			37		
Equatorial Guinea	108	48.4 / 51.6			178		
Fiji	20	70.6 / 74.9	128 / 128	64 / 65	48	41	35
French Polynesia	11	69.3 / 74.6	118 / 113	69 / 86	68		
Gambia	122	45.4 / 48.6	87 / 67	30 / 19	155	12	7
Guadaloupe	9	73.6 / 80.9			29	44	31
Guam	10	73.0 / 77.4			96		
Guyana	58	61.1 / 67.9	95 / 94	73 / 78	58	31	28
Iceland	5	76.8 / 81.3	98 / 98	105 / 103	24		
Luxembourg	7	73.3 / 79.9			12		
Maldives	50	65.7 / 63.3	130 / 127	49 / 49	54		
Malta	8	74.9 / 79.3	108 / 107	86 / 80	12		
Martinique	7	75.5 / 82.0			27	51	37
Micronesia (26)	34	67.6 / 71.4			56		
Netherlands Antilles	14	72.5 / 78.4			35		
Polynesia (27)	17	69.3 / 74.2			55		
Qatar	17	70.0 / 75.4	87 / 86	80 / 79	66	32	29
Reunion	9	70.9 / 79.8			20	67	62
Samoa	23	69.3 / 73.6	106 / 100	59 / 66	37		
Solomon Islands	23	69.7 / 73.9	103 / 89	21 / 14	94		
Suriname	29	67.5 / 72.7			22		
Swaziland	65	57.9 / 62.5	122 / 115	55 / 54	90	20	17

Demographic, Social and Economic Indicators

	Total population (thousands) 1999	Projected population (thousands) 2025	% urban (1995)	Urban growth rate (1995-2000)	Total fertility rate (1995-2000)	% births with skilled attendants	GNP per capita PPP$ (1997)	Under-5 mortality M / F
Bahamas	301	415	86.5	1.9	2.60	100		20 / 15
Bahrain	606	858	90.3	2.7	2.90	98		26 / 17
Barbados	269	297	47.4	1.7	1.50	98		14 / 15
Brunei Darussalam	322	459	57.8	2.2	2.80	98		11 / 11
Cape Verde	418	671	54.3	5.5	3.56		2,950	68 / 60
Comoros	676	1,176	30.7	5.6	4.80	52	1,530	112 / 101
Cyprus	778	900	54.1	1.9	2.03	98		10 / 9
Djibouti	629	1,026	82.8	2.6	5.30	79		182 / 166
East Timor	871	1,185	7.5	1.7	4.35			205 / 196
Equatorial Guinea	442	795	42.2	5.2	5.58	5		184 / 169
Fiji	806	1,104	40.7	2.5	2.73	100	3,860	28 / 18
French Polynesia	231	324	56.4	2.2	2.85	98		14 / 14
Gambia	1,268	2,151	25.5	5.3	5.20	44	1,440	212 / 194
Guadaloupe	450	569	99.4	1.6	1.90			12 / 9
Guam	164	228	38.2	2.4	3.40	100		11 / 13
Guyana	855	1,045	36.2	2.9	2.32	93	2,800	90 / 65
Iceland	279	328	91.6	1.2	2.10	100		6 / 6
Luxembourg	426	463	89.1	1.4	1.67	100		8 / 8
Maldives	278	501	26.8	4.3	5.40	90	3,340	53 / 80
Malta	386	430	89.3	0.9	1.89	98	13,380	11 / 8
Martinique	392	450	93.3	1.3	1.75			10 / 8
Micronesia (26)	530	960	42.7	3.2	4.08			47 / 40
Netherlands Antilles	215	258	69.5	1.3	2.20	98		20 / 12
Polynesia (27)	621	909	41.3	2.6	3.38			20 / 21
Qatar	589	779	91.4	2.1	3.74	97		27 / 18
Reunion	691	880	67.8	2.3	2.10	97		11 / 9
Samoa	177	271	21.0	2.4	4.15	52	3,570	25 / 29
Solomon Islands	430	817	17.1	6.3	4.85	85	2,270	32 / 22
Suriname	415	525	50.4	2.5	2.21	91		39 / 28
Swaziland	980	1,785	31.2	5.7	4.70	56	3,690	109 / 91

Notes for Indicators

The designations employed in this publication do not imply the expression of any opinion on the part of the United Nations Population Fund concerning the legal status of any country, territory or area or of its authorities, or concerning the delimitation of its frontiers or boundaries.

Data for small countries or areas, generally those with population of 200,000 or less in 1990, are not given in this table separately. They have been included in their regional population figures.

(*) More-developed regions comprise North America, Japan, Europe and Australia-New Zealand.

(+) Less-developed regions comprise all regions of Africa, Latin America and Caribbean, Asia (excluding Japan), and Melanesia, Micronesia and Polynesia.

(‡) Least-developed countries according to standard United Nations designation.

(1) Including British Indian Ocean Territory and Seychelles.

(2) Including Agalesa, Rodrigues and St. Brandon.

(3) Including Sao Tome and Principe.

(4) Formerly Zaire.

(5) Including Western Sahara.

(6) Including St. Helena, Ascension and Tristan da Cunha.

(7) Including Macau.

(8) On 1 July 1997, Hong Kong became a Special Administrative Region of China.

(9) Including Gaza Strip (Palestine).

(10) Turkey is included in Western Asia for geographical reasons. Other classifications include this country in Europe.

(11) Including Channel Islands, Faeroe Islands and Isle of Man.

(12) Including Andorra, Gibraltar, Holy See and San Marino.

(13) Including Leichtenstein and Monaco.

(14) Including Anguilla, Antigua and Barbuda, Aruba, British Virgin Islands, Cayman Islands, Dominica, Grenada, Montserrat, Netherlands Antilles, Saint Kitts and Nevis, Saint Lucia, Saint Vincent and the Grenadines, Turks and Caicos Islands, and United States Virgin Islands.

(15) Including Falkland Islands (Malvinas) and French Guiana.

(16) Including Bermuda, Greenland, and St. Pierre and Miquelon.

(17) Including Christmas Island, Cocos (Keeling) Islands and Norfolk Island.

(18) Including New Caledonia and Vanuatu.

(19) The successor States of the former USSR are grouped under existing regions. Eastern Europe includes Belarus, Republic of Moldova, Russian Federation and Ukraine. Western Asia includes Armenia, Azerbaijan and Georgia. South Central Asia includes Kazakhstan, Kyrgyzstan, Tajikistan, Turkmenistan and Uzbekistan.

(20) Regional total, excluding subregion reported separately below.

(21) These subregions comprise the UNFPA Arab States and Europe region.

(22) Estimates based on previous years' reports. Updated data are expected.

(23) Total for Eastern Europe includes some South European Balkan States and Northern European Baltic States.

(24) This figure includes Belgium and Luxembourg.

(25) More recent reports suggest this figure might have been higher. Future publications will reflect the evaluation of this information.

(26) Comprising Federated States of Micronesia, Guam, Kiribati, Marshall Islands, Nauru, Northern Mariana Islands, Pacific Islands (Palau) and Wake Island.

(27) Comprising American Samoa, Cook Islands, Johnston Island, Pitcairn, Samoa, Tokelau, Tonga, Midway Islands, Tuvalu, and Wallis and Futuna Islands.

Technical Notes

The statistical tables in this year's *State of World Population* report once again give special attention to indicators that can help track progress in meeting the quantitative and qualitative goals of the International Conference on Population and Development in the areas of mortality reduction, access to education, and access to reproductive health services, including family planning. Future reports will include different process measures when these become available, as ICPD follow-up efforts lead to improved monitoring systems. Improved monitoring of the financial contributions of governments, non-governmental organizations and the private sector should also allow better future reporting of expenditures and resource mobilization for ICPD implementation efforts. The sources for the indicators and their rationale for selection follow, by category.

Monitoring ICPD goals

Indicators of Mortality

Infant mortality, male and female life expectancy at birth. Source: United Nations Population Division. (Forthcoming.) *World Population Prospects: The 1998 Revision* (Data diskettes, "Demographic Indicators 1950-2050"). New York: United Nations. These indicators are measures of mortality levels, respectively, in the first year of life (which is most sensitive to development levels) and over the entire lifespan.

Maternal mortality ratio. Source: Data compiled from WHO, UNICEF, the World Bank and national sources as published in The World Bank. 1999. *World Development Indicators 1999.* Washington, D.C.: Oxford Press. This indicator presents the number of deaths to women per 100,000 live births which result from conditions related to pregnancy, delivery and related complications. Precision is difficult, though relative magnitudes are informative. Estimates below 50 are not rounded; those 50-100 are rounded to the nearest 5; 100-1,000, to the nearest 10; and above 1,000, to the nearest 100. Several of the estimates differ from official government figures. The estimates are based on reported figures wherever possible, using approaches to improve the comparability of information from different sources. See the source for details on the origin of particular national estimates. Estimates and methodologies are being reviewed by WHO, UNICEF, UNFPA, academic institutions and other agencies and will be revised where necessary, as part of the ongoing process of improving maternal mortality data. Future reports may give a range for adjusted estimates and original national source data.

Indicators of Education

Male and female gross primary enrolment ratios, male and female gross secondary enrolment ratios. Source: Spreadsheets provided by UNESCO; data published in the *World Education Report* series. Paris: UNESCO. Gross enrolment ratios indicate the number of students enrolled in a level in the education system per 100 individuals in the appropriate age group. They do not correct for individuals who are older than the level-appropriate age due to late starts, interrupted schooling or grade repetition.

Male and female adult illiteracy. Source: Spreadsheets provided by UNESCO; data published in the *Education for All: Status and Trends* series; Paris: UNESCO. Illiteracy definitions are subject to variation in different countries; three widely accepted definitions are in use. In so far as possible, data refer to the proportion who cannot, with understanding, both read and write a short simple statement on everyday life. Adult illiteracy (rates for persons above 15 years of age) reflects both recent levels of educational enrolment and past educational attainment. The above education indicators have been updated using the UN Population Division estimates from *World Population Prospects (The 1998 Revision)*. Education data are most recent, ranging from 1982-1996.

Per cent reaching grade 5 of primary education. Source: Spreadsheets provided by UNESCO; data published in the *World Education Report* series; Paris: UNESCO. Studies of patterns of dropout show high consistency between completing 5th grade and completing primary school. We report the former, following our source (identified as "Survival rate to grade 5"). Data are most recent within the years 1980-1995.

Indicators of Reproductive Health

Contraceptive knowledge. Source: United Nations Population Division. 1996. *World Population Monitoring 1996*. New York: United Nations. These indicators, derived from sample survey reports, estimate the proportion of women who have knowledge of a method of family planning and know a source from which contraceptives can be obtained. All contracep-

tive methods (medical, barrier, natural and traditional) are included in the first indicator; source information is more relevant to medical and barrier contraceptives and to modern periodic abstinence methods. These numbers are generally but not completely comparable across countries due to variation in populations surveyed by age (15- to 49-year-old women being most common) and marital status (e.g., currently or ever-married women, or all women) and in the timing of the surveys. Most of the data were collected during 1987-1994.

Births per 1,000 women aged 15-19. Source: United Nations Population Division. (Forthcoming.) *World Population Prospects: The 1998 Revision* (Data diskettes, "Demographic Indicators 1950-2050"); and United Nations Population Division. 1998. *Age Patterns of Fertility: The 1998 Revision*. New York: United Nations. This is an indicator of the burden of fertility on young women. Since it is an annual level summed over all women in the age cohort, it does not reflect fully the level of fertility for women during their youth. Since it indicates the annual average number of births per woman per year, one could multiply it by five to approximate the number of births to 1,000 young women during their late teen years. The measure does not indicate the full dimensions of teen pregnancy as only live births are included in the numerator. Stillbirths and spontaneous or induced abortions are not reflected.

Contraceptive prevalence. Source: United Nations Population Division. 1998. *Contraceptive Trends and Levels 1998* (wallchart). New York: United Nations. These data are derived from sample survey reports and estimate the proportion of married women (including women in consensual unions) currently using, respectively, any method or modern methods of contraception. Modern or clinic and supply methods include male and female sterilization, IUD, the pill, injectables, hormonal implants, condoms and female barrier methods. These numbers are roughly but not completely comparable across countries due to variation in populations surveyed by age (15- to 49 year old women being most common; slightly more than half of the database), in the timing of the surveys, and in the details of the questions. All of the data were collected in 1975 or later. The most recent survey data available are cited; nearly 80 per cent of the data refer to the period 1987-1996.

Demographic, Social and Economic Indicators

Total population 1999, projected population 2025, average annual population growth rate for 1995-2000. Source: United Nations Population Division. (Forthcoming.) *World Population Prospects: The 1998 Revision.* (Data diskettes, "Demographic Indicators 1950-2050"); and United Nations Population Division. 1998. *Annual Populations 1950-2050: The 1998 Revision.* New York: United Nations. These indicators present the size, projected future size and current period annual growth of national populations.

Per cent urban, urban growth rates. Source: United Nations Population Division. 1996. *World Urbanization Prospects: The 1996 Revision.* New York: United Nations. These indicators reflect the proportion of the national population living in urban areas and the growth rate in urban areas projected for 1995-2000.

Agricultural population per hectare of arable and permanent crop land. Source: Data provided by Food and Agriculture Organization, using agricultural population data based on the total populations from United Nations Population Division. (Forthcoming.) *World Population Prospects: The 1998 Revision.* New York: United Nations. This indicator relates the size of the agricultural population to the land suitable for agricultural production. It is responsive to changes in both the structure of national economies (proportions of the workforce in agriculture) and in technologies for land development. High values can be related to stress on land productivity and to fragmentation of land holdings. However, the measure is also sensitive to differing development levels and land use policies.

Total fertility rate (period: 1995-2000). Source: United Nations Population Division. (Forthcoming.) *World Population Prospects: The 1998 Revision.* (Data diskettes, "Demographic Indicators 1950-2050".) New York: United Nations. The measure indicates the number of children a woman would have during her reproductive years if she bore children at the rate estimated for different age groups in the specified time period. Countries may reach the projected level at different points within the period.

Access to basic care. Note: This indicator has been omitted from this year's report due to interagency concern about its reliability and validity. Consultations about an appropriate alternate indicator of access to health care are planned.

Births with skilled attendants. Source: World Health Organization; updated information provided by WHO. This indicator is based on national reports of the proportion of births attended by "skilled health personnel or skilled attendant: doctors (specialist or non-specialist) and/or persons with midwifery skills who can diagnose and manage obstetrical complications as well as normal deliveries". Data estimates are the most recent available.

Gross national product per capita. Source: 1997 figures from: The World Bank. 1999. *World Development Indicators 1999.* Washington, D.C.: The World Bank. This indicator measures the total output of goods and services for final use produced by residents and non-residents, regardless of allocation to domestic and foreign claims, in relation to the size of the population. As such, it is an indicator of the economic productivity of a nation. It differs from gross domestic product by further adjusting for income received from abroad for labour and capital by residents, for similar payments to non-residents, and by incorporating various technical adjustments including those related to exchange rate changes over time. This measure also takes into account the differing purchasing power of currencies by including purchasing power parity (PPP) adjustments of "real GNP". Some PPP figures are based on regression models; others are extrapolated from the latest International Comparison Programme benchmark estimates; see original source for details.

Central government expenditures on education and health. Source: The World Bank. 1999. *World Development Indicators 1999.* Washington, D.C.: The World Bank. These indicators reflect the priority afforded to education and health sectors by a country through the government expenditures dedicated to them. They are not sensitive to differences in allocations within sectors, e.g., primary education or health services in relation to other levels, which vary considerably. Direct comparability is complicated by the different administrative and budgetary responsibilities allocated to central governments in relation to local governments, and to the varying roles of the private and public sectors. Reported estimates are calculated from source data on public education spending as a share of GNP, per capita health expenditures (in PPP adjusted dollars) and the share of health expenditure from public sources. Data refer to the most recent estimates 1990-1997.

External assistance for population. Source: UNFPA. (Forthcoming.) *Global Population Assistance Report 1997.* New York: UNFPA. This figure provides the amount of external assistance expended in 1997 for population activities in each country. External funds are disbursed through multilateral and bilateral assistance agencies and by non-governmental organizations. Donor countries are indicated by their contributions being placed in parentheses. Future editions of this report will use other indicators to provide a better basis for comparing and evaluating resource flows in support of population and reproductive health programmes from various national and international sources. Regional totals include both country-level projects and regional activities (not otherwise reported in the table).

Under-5 mortality. Source: United Nations Population Division, special tabulation based on United Nations. (Forthcoming.) *World Population Prospects: The 1998 Revision.* New York: United Nations. This indicator relates to the incidence of mortality to infants and young children. It reflects, therefore, the impact of diseases and other causes of death on infants, toddlers and young children. More standard demographic measures are infant mortality and mortality rates for 1 to 4 years of age, which reflect differing causes of and frequency of mortality in these ages. The measure is more sensitive than infant mortality to the burden of childhood diseases, including those preventable by improved nutrition and by immunization programmes. Under-5 mortality is here expressed as deaths to children under 5 per 1,000 live births in a given year. The estimate refers to the period 1995-2000.

Per capita energy consumption. Source: The World Bank. 1999. *World Development Indicators 1999*. Washington, D.C.: The World Bank. This indicator reflects annual consumption of commercial primary energy (coal, lignite, petroleum, natural gas and hydro, nuclear and geothermal electricity) in kilograms of oil equivalent per capita. It reflects the level of industrial development, the structure of the economy and patterns of consumption. Changes over time can reflect changes in the level and balance of various economic activities and changes in the efficiency of energy use (including decreases or increases in wasteful consumption).

Access to safe water. Source: WHO/UNICEF. *Water Supply and Sanitation Sector Monitoring Report 1996*. This indicator reports the percentage of the population with *access* to an *adequate amount* of *safe* drinking water located within a *convenient distance* from the user's dwelling. The italicized words use country-level definitions. It is related to exposure to health risks, including those resulting from improper sanitation. Data are from 1990-1994.

THE STATE OF WORLD POPULATION 1999

Editor: Alex Marshall

Research and Writing: Stan Bernstein

Editorial Research: Karen Hardee and Frederick A.B. Meyerson

Managing Editor: William A. Ryan

Editorial Assistant: Phyllis Brachman

Cover photo: Large inset of Vietnamese school girl—Jorgen Schytte/Still Pictures